Come In, Lord, Please Excuse the Mess!

Spiritual Healing & Recovery from Clutter Bondage

A MESSY-A.N.I.C GUIDE

CASSANDRA TIERSMA

Clearhaven Press

Copyright © 2019 by Cassandra Tiersma.
ISBN 978-1-7342331-0-0
All rights reserved.

No part of this publication may be reproduced, distributed or transmitted in any form or by any means, including photocopying, recording, or other electronic or mechanical methods, without the prior written permission of the copyright holder, except as permitted by USA copyright law.

All scripture quotations, unless otherwise noted, are taken from the Holy Bible, New Century Version®, copyright © 2005 by Thomas Nelson. Used by permission. All rights reserved.

Scripture quotations marked "NLT" are taken from the Holy Bible, New Living Translation®, copyright © 1996, 2004, 2015 by Tyndale House Foundation. Used by permission of Tyndale House Publishers, a Division of Tyndale House Ministries, Carol Stream, Illinois 60188. All rights reserved.

Scripture quotations marked "GNT" are from the Good News Translation in Today's English Version - Second Edition, copyright © 1992 by American Bible Society. Used by permission.

Scripture quotations marked "NKJV" are taken from the New King James Version. Copyright © 1982 by Thomas Nelson, Inc. Used by permission. All rights reserved.

Scripture quotations marked "NIV" are taken from the Holy Bible, New International Version®, NIV®. Copyright © 1973, 1978, 1984, 2011 by International Bible Society. Used by permission of Zondervan. All rights reserved worldwide.

Scripture quotations marked "CEV" are from the Contemporary English Version, copyright © 1991, 1992, 1995 by American Bible Society. Used by Permission.

Scripture quotations marked "RSV" are from the Revised Standard Version of the Bible, copyright 1952 [2nd edition, 1971] by the Division of Christian Education of the National Council of the Churches of Christ in the United States of America. Used by permission. All rights reserved.

Scripture quotations marked "CEB" are taken from the Common English Bible®, CEB® Copyright © 2010, 2011 by Common English Bible.™ Used by permission. All rights reserved worldwide.

Scriptures marked "CJB" are taken from the Complete Jewish Bible, copyright © 1998 by David H. Stern. Published by Jewish New Testament Publications, Inc. Used by permission. All rights reserved.

Scripture quotations marked "TLB" are taken from The Living Bible, © 1971. Used by permission of Tyndale House Publishers, a Division of Tyndale House Ministries, Carol Stream, Illinois 60188. All rights reserved.

Scripture Quotations marked "GWT" are taken from God's Word Translation, copyright © 1995 by God's Word to the Nations. Used by permission of Baker Publishing Group. All rights reserved.

Scripture quotations marked "CSB" are taken from the Christian Standard Bible®, copyright © 2017 by Holman Bible Publishers. Used by permission.

Cover Design by 100Covers.com
Interior Design by FormattedBooks.com

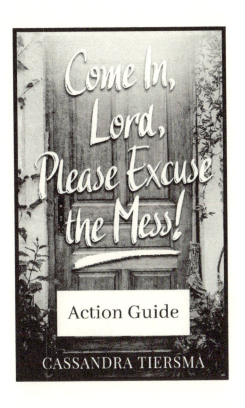

DOWNLOAD THE ACTION GUIDE
FREE!

READ THIS FIRST

Just to say thanks for buying my book, I would like to give you the ACTION GUIDE workbook 100% FREE!

TO DOWNLOAD, GO TO:
http://bit.ly/MessyanicActionGuide.

FOREWORD
By Ceci Garrett

*"So now there is no condemnation for
those who belong to Christ Jesus.
And because you belong to Him,
the power of the life-giving Spirit has freed you
from the power of sin that leads to death."*
—Romans 8:1-2 NLT

When I started offering workshops to individuals who struggled with collecting and saving habits, I was coming out of my own brokenness. In some misguided attempt to fix my childhood home, I desperately hoped that I might find a way to help others who were looking for help. "If only someone had offered my mom help," I'd rationalize, "perhaps, just perhaps, things might have been different for my family."

But God is faithful to heal those who seek Him. He is a good, good Father who heals in ways that we don't know how to ask. Even as I was being an instrument of hope and blessing to women like Cassandra, I was being healed by these candid and raw admissions. Like the ones being offered by Cassandra in this book. The same candid and raw admissions recounted through both the Old and New Testament. There is healing when we seek God to be in the mess with us.

I know that you will find Cassandra's personal story and strategies helpful as you invite Abba Father into the mess.

"Do not be afraid or discouraged,
for the Lord will personally go ahead of you.
He will be with you;
He will neither fail you nor abandon you."
—Deuteronomy 31:8 NLT

As you pick up this book, you are beginning a journey to finally move out of the past, out of the shame. As you go through this healing journey on your road to recovery, you may bump into some uncomfortable feelings. But you can be assured that Holy Spirit will walk with you. Jehovah Rapha, God is Healer, will bind up your broken heart if only you allow Him to have His way.

As you begin to approach the Throne of God, I encourage you to let go of your preconceived ideas of what healing looks like. Like prayer, healing often looks different than we expect, because God knows all and gives only His best to His beloved children. At times, healing in my own life has looked more like disaster and continued destruction. Likewise, I've seen homes appear to get worse during the processing of the excess. Have faith! Be of good courage! God is not done with you, your story, or your home yet.

Remember that, ultimately, what God asks of us is to pursue Him and our relationship with Him and His children. If that "treasure" does not bring God and your brothers and sisters in Christ closer to you, consider the sacrifice of letting it go to someone for whom it will.

Finally, it's been such an honor to be a part of Cassandra's walk with God and her continued healing from "clutter bondage." Often, part of healing is doing just this, sharing our story with those who it can encourage and help. "Come In, Lord, Please Excuse the Mess!" is a testimony of what God can do in the heart of a woman who seeks Him first—in the midst of the mess. It's my prayer that you will find hope and encouragement from Cassandra's struggles and that you'll consider sharing this book with those you know who are struggling ankle-

or waist-deep in their possessions. I can't wait to use this resource with those in my church and community!

Ceci Garrett
Christian writer/speaker, &
Professional Coach/Consultant
on clutter & hoarding tendencies,
& in-home therapeutic decluttering
https://www.facebook.com/CeciGarrett/

INTRODUCTION

If your idea of clutter is the day's mail on the kitchen counter and a stray pair of shoes under the coffee table, this book is NOT for you.

If you've never misplaced your keys, never had to pay a late fee on a utility bill, never had an overdue library fine because you lost a book, never had to send a belated birthday card because you kept forgetting to buy a stamp, or never forgotten to pick up something (or someone) when you were supposed to ... you've obviously wandered into the wrong book!

Come In, Lord, Please Excuse the Mess! was written by and for the "Messy-a.n.i.c." Christian woman—the *Messy, absent-minded, normal-ish, imperfect, creative* Christian woman—who struggles with chronic clutter. The Messy-a.n.i.c. Christian woman who, albeit jokingly, self-identifies as a domestically challenged, clutter-impaired, creative, messy person.

If you would rather shop than mop, sleep than sweep, scrapbook than clean crap and cook, or weed a bed of flowers than make the bed and clean the shower … if your idea of cleaning house is sweeping the room with a glance, this might be a book for you.

If you've ever been reluctant to invite someone into your home because of the disarray, if you'd rather go out for coffee than have someone over for coffee (because that's so much easier than tidying up the house), or if you've ever opted to eat somewhere else in the house besides the dining room (because it's quicker than having to clear the clutter off the table), and if you need at least a two-week notice before someone can drop over for an "unexpected" visit, then **Come In, Lord, Please Excuse the Mess!** is definitely for you.

WHAT THIS BOOK IS (AND WHAT IT ISN'T):

This is NOT another "how-to" organizational system for whipping clutter into shape once and for all. There are already resources out there for that. Besides, dealing with clutter isn't a one-and-done deal. Clutter is a recurring reality of active living. The more activities and interests you and your family are involved in, the more recurring opportunities there are for clutter challenges.

Come In, Lord, Please Excuse the Mess! IS a spiritual recovery book to help you break free from the mental, emotional, and physical strongholds of clutter bondage. I understand the pain and shame, the confusion and paralysis that come from living with a clutter disorder. I fully grasp these negative feelings that can so often prevent us from living the life we crave.

Each chapter addresses a specific spiritual breakthrough (such as Action, Readiness, Discernment, Freedom, Victory, Self-Control, Contentment, and many more). Corresponding prayers for a spiritual breakthrough are provided in every chapter, to help you invite the Lord into the heart of your struggle with clutter. As you strategically pray for genuine healing and transformation in the journey out of clutter bondage, He will change you from the inside out.

Every chapter will provide you with fresh, new insight into the cause of the problem, and guidelines on how to go about breaking the chains of clutter bondage through strategic prayer and action steps. As you turn to God for direction, this book will provide practical tips on how to resolve the problem of clutter bondage.

WHO I AM (AND WHO I AM NOT):

I am a Messy-a.n.i.c. Christian who has struggled with a clutter disorder for many years. But I have been able to experience spiritual healing and recovery from the debilitating effects of living with a clutter disorder, through prayer and the Word of God. Although I am not "cured" and I still struggle at times, I am no longer a spiritual cripple being held hostage to clutter. Thankfully, I am now living a fulfilling life, utilizing my God-given gifts and talents, to the glory of God—in spite of the mess!

The goal of this book is to enable you to do the same!

Throughout this book, I share deeply personal stories of my own struggles with clutter bondage and the spiritual journey of how God delivered me from the emotional pain and crippling anguish associated with clutter.

Prior to learning and applying the truths in this book, I used to feel like a hostage in my own home, too ashamed of my failure in the housekeeping department to feel worthy of serving the Lord as He was leading me. But as I spent time in the Word and in prayer, seeking God in the middle of my mess, the Holy Spirit changed me from the inside out. I was delivered from the crippling shame that held me in mental, emotional, and spiritual bondage to clutter.

By the power and grace of God, through the process outlined in this recovery guide, I was released into the abundant life that God had purposed for me! I now work as a professional writer, serve as the women's ministry director at my church, lead teen Bible study class, as well as serve in music and children's ministry.

HOW TO USE THIS BOOK:

This book can be read in a couple of ways. You can use it as …

- A one-month personal study by going through one chapter a day for four weeks (taking a Sabbath break each week).

- Or as a six-month weekly group study by going through one chapter a week for 26 weeks.

> To download
> **Group Study Format with Leader Guidelines,**
> go to: http://bit.ly/MessyanicActionGuide.

Whichever way you choose to use this book, if you will invite the Lord into your mess and work through this recovery study, I promise that you and your relationship to "stuff" will be permanently changed for the better.

My prayer is that, after reading this book, you will be able to hold your head high and walk confidently in the life God has purposed for you while enjoying a closer relationship with the One who created you and died for you. My prayer is that you can live the abundant life you were designed by God to live.

If you are ensnared by the chains of clutter bondage—feeling discouraged, frustrated, inadequate, and disabled—there is hope for you! You, too, can break free from the mental and emotional pain of clutter bondage. A spiritual breakthrough can be yours!

In working through this recovery book, you will be changed from the inside out. You will experience life-changing revelation about your struggle, and a deeper walk with the Lord as He leads you out of bondage into the life that He has planned for you.

So, get ready to open the door—not only to your home but also to your heart—and tell Him,

"Come In, Lord, Please Excuse the Mess!"

TABLE OF CONTENTS

FOREWORD	V
INTRODUCTION	IX

PART ONE—Opening the Door   1

Chapter 1: **Come In, Lord, Please Excuse the Mess!**   3
      Breakthrough in Humility

Chapter 2: **Taking Out the Trash**   9
      Breakthrough in Obedience

Chapter 3: **Getting Started**   19
      Breakthrough in Repentance

Chapter 4: **No More Shame**   27
      Breakthrough in Courage

Chapter 5: **Get More Done by Working Together**   37
      Breakthrough in Fellowship

Chapter 6: **Don't Fall Off Your Stick**   43
      Breakthrough in Sustenance

Chapter 7: **From Immobilized to Energized** 51
    Breakthrough in Action
Chapter 8: **Get Dressed** 59
    Breakthrough in Readiness
Chapter 9: **The Sea of Clutter** 65
    Breakthrough in Hope
Chapter 10: **Call Me Blessed** 69
    Breakthrough in Faith
Chapter 11: **In the Valley of Decision** 77
    Breakthrough in Discernment

PART TWO—Sweeping the Floor 85
Chapter 12: **Swept and Put in Order** 87
    Breakthrough in Purification
Chapter 13: **Captive No More** 95
    Breakthrough in Freedom
Chapter 14: **Defeating the Enemy** 99
    Breakthrough in Victory
Chapter 15: **When Clutter Becomes a Spiritual Battle** 107
    Breakthrough in Strength
Chapter 16: **Emotional Ties That Bind Us to Clutter** 113
    Breakthrough in Release
Chapter 17: **"Fuh Gedda Bow Dit"** 121
    Breakthrough in Relinquishment
Chapter 18: **From Avoidance to Forgiveness** 127
    Breakthrough in Compassion

Chapter 19: **Can't Take It with You**   137
        Breakthrough in Perspective

PART THREE—Saying No to More   147
Chapter 20: **More Than Enough**   149
        Breakthrough in Self-Control
Chapter 21: **Physical Preparedness vs.**
        Spiritual Readiness   155
        Breakthrough in Trust
Chapter 22: **Jesus Is My Superpower**   163
        Breakthrough in Dependence
Chapter 23: **A Pile to Remind Us**   171
        Breakthrough in Accessibility
Chapter 24: **I Have Everything I Need**   177
        Breakthrough in Contentment
Chapter 25: **The Wilderness of Sin**   181
        Breakthrough in Stages
Chapter 26: **Looking Forward to the**
        Future with Joy!   187
        Breakthrough in Recovery

ENDNOTES   195
More RESOURCES
for Spiritual Healing & Recovery   205
GRATITUDE   209
ABOUT THE AUTHOR   211
CAN YOU HELP?   213

PART ONE
Opening the Door

"I have a fond daydream of a day when, like normal, uncluttered folks, I can bring people through my house without hesitation, without secrecy, and without closed doors."
~ Eve O. Schaub,
Year of No Clutter

CHAPTER 1

"Come In, Lord, Please Excuse the Mess!"
Breakthrough in Humility

> "Lord, I am not worthy
> for You to come into my house."
> —from Matthew 8:8

Can you relate to those words of the army officer in Capernaum? Like this officer in Matthew 8, do you also feel a sense of shame or unworthiness about having someone come into your home?

I'm reluctant to admit this, but one time, many years ago, when my parents were visiting from out of state, I hosted a "garden party" family gathering at my home *without even inviting them into my house.* That's how embarrassed and ashamed I was about my problem with clutter.

I've struggled for years with what I call a "Clutter Disorder." I'm pretty sure I've read nearly every book written on the topics of clutter and disorganization. Additionally, I've taken several courses for dealing with clutter and chronic disorganization. I've been a member of multiple online support groups for women who share the same struggles with clutter.

The apostle Paul wrote of having a "thorn in the flesh" (a chronic, painful problem), and how he'd begged the Lord to take the problem away from him. Similarly, I have anguished over my "thorn in the flesh," my problem with ADD-related physical clutter, without relief. Paul concluded, however, that the Lord told him, **"My grace is enough for you. When you are weak, My power is made perfect in you"** (2 Corinthians 12:9).

Paul claimed the problem he struggled with had been given to him so that he would not become too proud. He said it was a messenger from Satan to beat him and to keep him from being too proud. Surprisingly, Paul said he was very happy to brag about his weakness.[1]

Although my ongoing secret struggle with clutter has definitely beat me and kept me from being too proud, it's not something I've been very happy to brag about. But, again, the Lord said, **"When you are weak, My power is made perfect in you."**

That's why Paul declared, "… **then Christ's power can live in me.**"

Every time I read those words in Second Corinthians 12:9, in which Christ promises that His power is made perfect in our own weaknesses, I thank God for my weakness—my painful *thorn-in-the-flesh* problem with clutter—because that is what led to my salvation.

About 17 years ago, desperate for help, I attended a weekend seminar called "The Industrious, Well-Organized, Proverbs 31 Woman." During a short break, I went up to the seminar instructor, a woman named Sydney Lander. She prayed with me and led me to Christ.

It was my concern about the condition of my house that had led me to the seminar, but God was concerned about something greater: the condition of my spiritual "house"—my soul. I wanted a tidy house. He wanted a relationship with me. The very thing that was my weakness, that had beaten me down, led me to Him—to a saving faith in Jesus Christ. That's why I thank God for my weakness. *It is because of my weakness* that "Christ's power can live in me."

Several years later, I read a devotional in the *Maximized Living Bible* that delved into the definition of the word "live" Paul used in Second Corinthians 12:9. When the apostle Paul wrote, **"Then Christ's power can live in me,"** author Dr. Ben Lerner explained that in Greek it meant, "to pitch a tent in." Paul was a tentmaker by trade, so we can assume he could have pitched a tent anywhere he wanted to. But it was his own self-confessed problem, or weakness, that made it possible for God "to pitch a tent in" Paul's heart. Dr. Lerner wrote, "... God lives in us, inside the tent He makes in the place where we were unable to cleanse ourselves."[2]

As homemakers, we often feel bad about ourselves because we think we should be able to get our "tent" in order. Like the army officer who said, **"Lord, I am not worthy for you to come into my house"** (Matthew 8:8), we may feel our home is "unworthy" to invite Jesus in. How can we expect to invite the Lord Jesus, or anyone else for that matter, into our home when even we feel uncomfortable with the state it's in? Dr. Lerner points out that, ironically, *"Jesus is at home where you feel out of place!"*[3]

We'd like to have all our things pulled together in a "Better Homes & Gardens" kind of way. But there's so much that needs doing. The bottom line? We need help in our struggle with clutter. Fortunately, *"God dwells in the midst of need,"* Dr. Lerner tells us. *"And the reason God doesn't remove that need is because that's His home."* Lerner adds, *"Jesus resides in those places where you are least com-*

fortable with your life—where you long to straighten things up and clean house."[4]

So, know that Jesus cares more about the condition of your *heart* than the condition of your *house*. Instead of saying, **"Lord, I am not worthy for You to come into my house,"**[5] invite Him in.

Honestly and humbly tell Him, **"Come in, Lord, please excuse the mess,"** and receive Him into your heart and home.

Tell Jesus:
Come in, Lord, please excuse the mess!

PRAYER

Thank You, Lord, that when I am weak, Your power is made perfect in me. Thank You for my weakness, my struggle with clutter. Help me to understand that You dwell in the midst of my need.

Thank You, Jesus, for caring more about the state of my heart than about the state of my house. Help me to care more about my relationship with You than about all of my stuff. Thank You for pitching a tent in my heart. Amen.

TAKE ACTION

- If Jesus walked into your house through the front door, what's the first thing He would see that would cause you embarrassment? Write it down here:

- Take a positive action step towards dealing with that item or area first. Make a plan, write it down on your calendar, and do it. (If you are physically unable to do it yourself, come up with a way to get the help of someone else to do it for you.)

- When it's done, come back to this page and write: *"Done!"* Sign your name here and write the date it was completed:

Read Chapter 2 for some nitty-gritty trash talk.

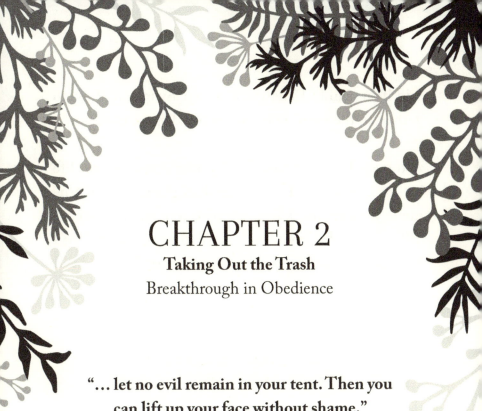

CHAPTER 2
Taking Out the Trash
Breakthrough in Obedience

"… let no evil remain in your tent. Then you can lift up your face without shame."
—Job 11:14b-15a

After I got saved at "The Industrious, Well-Organized, Proverbs 31 Woman" seminar, I began to feel uncomfortable about some of the things in my home. These things were from my life before Christ and no longer seemed to fit.

I didn't know what to do, so I called Sydney, the seminar instructor. I vaguely explained my dilemma, without being too specific. But Sydney asked me point-blank, "You mean things pertaining to witchcraft?" Although I'd never thought of those items in that way, when she said it so plainly, I knew it was true. Sydney told me to gather up the items in question and dispose of them.

Although I had not told Sydney anything about my life before Christ, the Holy Spirit had given her discernment without my having to give any specific details. What she didn't know was, prior to being saved, I had been deeply involved in all forms of what I later realized had been witchcraft—including metaphysics, the New Age Movement, the occult, Wicca, and shamanism.

I had been involved in numerology and had worked as a psychic on the Psychic Hotline, doing numerology readings for people all over the country. I was twice ordained, in two different "spiritual" organizations. I was a Reiki master and a T'ai Chi *sifu* (teacher.) My writing had been published in a national New Age metaphysical newspaper. I had been considered a "priestess" and had performed pagan wedding ceremonies. I had also served as a ceremonial leader for a women's circle that met monthly in a nearby large city.

I had even formed a secular women's circle in the small town where I was living at the time. I had presented and led women's "spiritual" retreats and had been a speaker and workshop presenter at Women of Vision & Action (WOVA) conferences in Coeur d'Alene, Idaho, and for the University of Oklahoma's Native Wellness & Spirituality Conference in Tucson, Arizona.

The tools of my (former) trade included certain books, tarot cards, runes, a crystal ball, smudge fan, Indian ceremonial pipe, and more. Those were the items that I needed to get out of my "tent." I boxed them all up, then called the secretary at the Four-Square Church I was attending and told her the situation—that I needed to get the items out of my house, but didn't want to just donate them to a thrift store where they could still be put into use. She wisely suggested I bring the box of stuff and leave it in the church's dumpster, which had a locked fence around it. That way, she assured me, it would all be burned. At that time, the city where we lived had a waste-to-energy plant with a massive incinerator.

I immediately took that box—filled with what I had come to know was "evil"—and deposited it into the church's secured dumpster, to be incinerated. When I got back in my car and was driving home, I suddenly cried out involuntarily, from deep within my spirit, "DADDY!" Tears of joy streamed down my face as I sobbed in grateful relief from having been cleansed, delivered, and restored to my Heavenly Father—Abba Daddy—God.

> **And because we are his children,
> God has sent the Spirit of his Son into our hearts,
> prompting us to call out, "Abba, Father."**
> —Galations 4:6-7, NLT

The first biblical account of a hoarder is in the Book of Genesis.[1] What's more, the items being hoarded were the Bible days' equivalent of that box of divination tools that I had to get rid of after I was saved. Before Jacob and his household fled from his unscrupulous father-in-law, Laban, Jacob's favorite wife, Rachel, stole her father's household idols. She stashed her hoard of pagan idols inside her camel's saddle to hide them. That secret stash of household gods, or talismans, isn't very different from some of the stuff we hold onto "just in case." Spiritually speaking, Rachel's hoard of little gods was trash—evil that that should have been destroyed and discarded.

There are certain home-keeping tasks that I find particularly distasteful, and they are the "icky" ones. Things having to do with yucky garbage cans and nasty kitty litter boxes. But the one I always dread is cleaning out the produce drawer in the bottom of the fridge. Invariably, there's something in the bottom of the drawer that I forgot about, turning to liquid slime. Besides serving as a shameful reminder of my ADD-related absent-mindedness, it's just plain gross!

There are plenty of things in daily life that are icky, nasty or gross—things that can't be avoided. But evil is a whole other story.

People who live in locations where they might encounter venomous snakes or large, poisonous insects might consider those to be "evil." My sister lives in the Sierra Nevada foothills, where rattlesnakes live. She had been in the habit of calling her adult son to come over every time a rattlesnake showed up on her driveway or near her house so that he could kill it for her. But one time recently, she impulsively grabbed a shovel and killed the snake herself. Not an easy feat—chopping off a rattlesnake's head with the pointed tip of a shovel blade.

Evil, like that rattlesnake's head, must be cut off. It can't be left lurking around the house.

Is there anything that you've ever had to discard because it was "evil?" Perhaps a video or DVD? Or a certain book? If so, how did you feel after you'd gotten rid of it?

Who takes out the trash at your house? Who took out the trash when you were growing up? Isn't it comforting to know that we have a heavenly Daddy, our Father God, who wants to take care of the "trash" in our life? No matter how icky, yucky, nasty, slimy or gross, He wants us to let Him take the spiritual "trash"—the evil—out of our lives.

There's a terrific "trash talk" poem by famous artist/poet, Shel Silverstein, in his book, *Where the Sidewalk Ends*. "Sarah Cynthia Sylvia Stout Would Not Take the Garbage Out" is an outlandish tale about a girl who refused to take out the trash.[2] I love the over-the-top silliness of it. Sadly, it's not just a funny, nonsensical rhyme in the lives of some people. There really are people who never take the garbage out.

My decluttering coach, Ceci Garrett, founder of "Lightening the Load" ministry, grew up with a mother who was a hoarder.[3] By the time Ceci was grown and married with children of her own, her mother's declining physical health and her hoarding illness had gotten to the point where she was living (or rather, dying) in filth. Her home had basically become a giant trash receptacle piled with meaningless clutter, trash, and soiled diapers. The situation was so extreme that she was featured in an episode of *Hoarders*. It was a real-life tragedy.

By the grace of God, through massive intervention efforts, Ceci was able to get her mother the medical care she needed and help place her in a safe, clutter-free, assisted-living home where she could begin to have a quality life again.

That real-life story may be an extreme example of what can happen when we don't deal with our mess, but it's also a good reminder that there can be life after clutter.

> **"We should remove from our lives anything that would get in the way and the sin that so easily holds us back."**
> —Hebrews 12:1b

> **"You give me a better way to live ..."**
> —Psalm 18:36a

PRAYER

Thank You, Father God, that You do not leave us wallowing in the filth, debris, and trash of our past choices. Thank You for taking the evil "trash" out of our lives and throwing it into the fiery inferno. Don't let me be like Jacob's wife, Rachel, hiding secret idols.[4]

Give me Holy Spirit discernment to recognize if there is anything in my home or life that You consider evil, which I should get rid of. Give me the emotional fortitude to remove and discard anything that is not pleasing to You, Lord. Let no evil remain in my tent, Lord, so I can lift my face toward You without shame. In Jesus' Name, amen.

TAKE ACTION

If Jesus was going to be house-sitting for you in your absence, is there anything in your home you would want to get rid of before His arrival? Is there any substance, literature, or object in your house that God might consider evil or unclean?

Ask the Holy Spirit to show you if there is anything that you need to get rid of. This is not about legalism. It's about your heart and obedience to God. If the Holy Spirit has brought something to mind, which you know you need to get rid of, go now and discard whatever it is. Put it in the trash. Then come back and write it down here:

NOTE

Even children can be involved in picking up trash and taking out the garbage. This practice can not only teach them valuable lessons in cleanliness, but also help them develop habits that will minimize clutter. For instance, on a list of age-appropriate chores for children, I found the following:

- "Throw trash away" is listed under ages 2-3.[5]
- "Pick up trash around the house" is listed under chores for 4-year-olds.[6]
- "Empty small wastebaskets" is listed under chores for children 4-5 years of age.[7]
- "Take out the garbage" and "Take out the trash" is listed under appropriate jobs for 6-8-year-old children.[8,9]

> **"Because the Lord your God walks
> in the midst of your camp,
> to save you and to give up your enemies before you,
> therefore your camp must be holy,
> that He may not see anything indecent among you,
> and turn away from you."**
> —Deuteronomy 23:14

(Messy-a.n.i.c. Praise Report: Since writing this chapter, I tackled the dreaded produce drawer in the bottom of my fridge. To expedite the task, rather than trying to weed

through the mess, I just had my husband dump its entire contents into the trash bin outside. I then sprayed the inside of the drawer with my favorite sanitizing, odor-neutralizing cleaner—hydrogen peroxide—and let it sit for a while. After allowing that to sit and do its magic, I wiped the drawer out with paper towels. To this day, my fridge no longer has any more mysterious odors, and the drawer remains clean and mostly empty, except for an onion at the moment. Praise the Lord!)

Note: Refrigerator drawers for fresh produce can be the bane of Messy-a.n.i.c. cooks, for out-of-sight-out-of-mind veggies are too oft forgotten until they are inedible. The solution to this recurring problem is to simply come to terms with the fact that, unless something is going to be consumed immediately, there is no point in stocking a produce drawer with good intentions that will inevitably become fodder for the compost bin. For the Messy-a.n.i.c. cook, it is a cleaner, less wasteful choice to stick with frozen, canned, and dried foods that will not decompose and smell up the fridge if not immediately consumed. Problem solved.)

Read Chapter 3: **Getting Started** to find out the most important, but most overlooked, biblical step in how to start the decluttering process.

CHAPTER 3
Getting Started
Breakthrough in Repentance

*"Show me what I should do,
because my prayers go up to You."*
—Psalm 143:8b

The hardest part of getting started on the decluttering process is knowing what to do, specifically *where to begin*. Consider these different recommendations, and think about what might work for you:

WHAT TO DO

- Start with a small, doable task so you'll be able to enjoy an immediate sense of accomplishment.
- Tackle that which causes you the most frustration and angst; once it's done, everything else will seem so much easier.

- Take one large decluttering project and break it down into small, manageable tasks.
- Set a timer for 15 minutes and do as much as you can until the timer goes off.
- Dump everything of one category of items (such as clothes, dishes, books, etc.) out onto the floor/table/bed, and pick up one item at a time, deciding whether to keep or discard it. Repeat the process until it's done.

WHERE TO START

- Start at the front door and work your way around the room (either clockwise or counterclockwise), repeating this process in each room.
- Start in the kitchen because that's the heart of the home.
- Start with the bathroom because it's the first room you visit when you wake up each morning.
- Start with the bedroom because it should be your sanctuary space. You want it to be a peaceful, stress-free zone for relaxing and going to sleep at the end of the day.
- Some say it doesn't matter *where* you start, just so long as you *start*.

In an attempt to get a clear idea on how and where to get started on decluttering, we read books on the subject; we enroll in workshops, seminars, and online courses; and we watch training videos by experts on organization. Some of us even join online support groups where we can interact among a safe group of other people who are also wondering how and where to get started.

But David, the author of the Book of Psalms, had the right idea. He consulted with his Heavenly Father, asking *Him* what he should do:

> **"Show me what I should do, because**
> **my prayers go up to You."**
> —Psalm 143:8b

When you need advice, to whom do you typically turn? Did you know that God is the Supreme Authority on project management? The God of the universe who created the world, who gave Noah the specifications for how to build the ark,[1] and who gave Moses meticulous instructions for how to build the Tabernacle,[2] can surely show you and me what to do to declutter our homes.

Our God is the Master Strategist who gave instructions for countless successful battle plans throughout the Old Testament, and who inspired and oversaw Nehemiah's rebuilding of the wall around Jerusalem.[3] He can certainly help us with a strategy for undertaking the process of restoring order to our homes.

We can take a lesson from Nehemiah, one of the greatest project managers in the Bible. Nehemiah had a burden on his heart to rebuild the wall of Jerusalem because he was so heartbroken for the Jewish people living in captivity, full of shame, amidst the rubble of the broken-down wall of Jerusalem.[4] Nehemiah's big project was essentially rebuilding—creating order out of the wreckage and devastation of previous years.[5]

The first thing Nehemiah did was pray to God, confessing the sins of his people.[6] He then verbalized his plan to the king of Persia when the king asked him, "What do you want?" Before responding, he prayed to God in order to receive His help and guidance for the task ahead.[7] His next step was to "set a time"[8] and to state what materials he would need to accomplish such a huge undertaking.[9] Once at the job site, Nehemiah did a "walk-through," assessing the damage, to get an idea of what all needed to be done.[10]

God shows us what to do. It is outlined in His Word. The first step is modeled by Nehemiah when he began with confession. He came before God and confessed his own sins and the sins of the people against God.[11] This spiritual step is usually overlooked by those who are embarking on the decluttering process.

Your reaction to this step might be something like, "What do I have to confess? I didn't willfully set out to create all this clutter and chaos. I'm just a victim of my circumstances." It may seem counterintuitive to confess sins that led to the current state of affairs, but the truth is that we do have a role in how things got to the point where they are now.

If you're wondering what kind of sins might need to be confessed, consider …

- The sin of over-busyness—not taking a weekly sabbath break from buying/shopping, constant doing, always being on the go, or surfing the Internet—without stopping regularly to just rest and be quiet, praying and listening to God.

> **"Remember to observe the Sabbath day by keeping it holy."**
> —Exodus 20:8, NLT

> **"The person who obeys the laws of the Sabbath will be blessed."**
> —Isaiah 56:2a

- The sin of discontentment—never being satisfied, never telling ourselves "no" whenever we see something that we think we can't live without, instead of setting and sticking to reasonable boundaries as to how much we actually need.

"Maybe so, but I say it is better to be content with what little you have. Otherwise, you will always be struggling for more, and that is like chasing the wind."
—Ecclesiastes 4:6

- The sin of fear—fear of running out of needed items, which can lead to "stocking up" more stuff than we can reasonably store or use—because we don't trust God to truly take care of us and provide for our needs.

"No, the Lord is all I need. He takes care of me."
—Psalm 16:5

"Jesus said to His followers, 'So I tell you, don't worry about the food you need to live, or about the clothes you need for your body.'"
—Luke 12:22

"The Lord is my Shepherd; I have everything I need."
—Psalm 23:1

Let's follow Nehemiah's example, now, by going to God in prayer. As you confess and repent, you can depend on God to help you decide where to start and what to do in order to "build your wall" and get your house in order.

PRAYER

Lord, in looking at the rubble of my life—all the clutter and especially cascading piles of paper clutter everywhere I turn—I remember Your servant, Nehemiah.

Nehemiah turned to You before undertaking his big project of rebuilding and creating order out of the wreckage of the wall around the city of Jerusalem. This means I can turn to You and Your Word for step-by-step instructions on how to go about the "clean-up" and restoration here, within the walls of my house.

Forgive me, Lord, for my part in creating or contributing to the cluttered state of my home. Forgive me for being too busy, without taking adequate sabbatical breaks to rest, recharge, and spend quiet time alone with You in prayer, reading my Bible, and listening for Your Voice. Please also forgive me for my lack of faith in Your ability to provide for all my needs, which led me to this position of having acquired too much stuff. I repent of having been dissatisfied with what You've already given me, always wanting to buy/get/have more. You are all I need, Lord. Thank You for taking care of me.

When there's so much that needs to be done, Lord, without You, I wouldn't even know where to start. I have such trouble with self-discipline, priorities, and boundaries. God, I need Your constant guidance. As I embark on this decluttering journey, show me what to do, Lord; my prayers go up to You. In Jesus' Name. Amen.

TAKE ACTION

Tell God what you want and why. Be specific. (For example: *"I want to have an orderly, clutter-free home so I can host weekly Bible studies."* Or, *"I want to pare down my possessions so I can always find what I need without wasting so much time trying to find lost items."* Or, *"I want to clear out the spare room so I can make it into a playroom for my grandkids."*)

Write down your "what" and "why" here:

Read Chapter 4: **No More Shame**
for a *Breakthrough in Courage!*

CHAPTER 4
No More Shame
Breakthrough in Courage

"Don't be afraid, because you will not be ashamed.
Don't be embarrassed, because
you will not be disgraced.
You will forget the shame you felt earlier…"
—Isaiah 54:4a

One of the most intimidating things about the whole decluttering challenge is the fear of being "found out"—of allowing someone else a real-life, up-close view of the chaotic clutter we can never seem to get a handle on.

As someone who has lived with this challenge for years, and who has been a participating member of several online support groups for the same issue, I know from personal experience that a great many of us are afraid to ask for help for fear of what others will think. And yet, we *need* help. We can't do it all on our own.

When God gave the prophet Isaiah the words in the scripture verse above, He was talking to His people in Jerusalem. In the previous two chapters of Isaiah, the Lord had given Isaiah a prophetic message about the coming Messiah who would be crucified so that we could be forgiven for our sins.[1] Then in the next chapter, God let them know that things were going to get better for them, that He was going to do a work in their midst. He promised salvation, restoration, and ultimate victory.[2]

The entire book of Isaiah is such a message of hope, not only for the nation of Israel but also for us. For we, too, are His children. The Lord God loves you and cares about you and your struggles and challenges, every bit as much as He loves and cares for Israel. So, when we read His Love Letter to us, called the Holy Bible, we can be comforted by the promise in the scripture verse above, which assures us victory through Christ.

Our victory in the battle against clutter and chaos comes not by our power, but by the power of God.

> **"'Their victory comes from Me,' says the Lord."**
> —Isaiah 54:17d

This means we can even have victory in Christ over the secret shame and embarrassment we've suffered because of our struggle with clutter. Still, it will take courage on our part to be honest about the state of our home.

There was one man in the Bible who made a mistake in disclosing the full contents of his home to an outsider. That was King Hezekiah when he showed the entire inventory of all his storehouses, all his wealth, all his treasure—"everything in his palace and in his kingdom"—to visiting messengers of his rival, the king of Babylon.[3] The margin note I'd jotted in my Bible next to that verse, from an earlier reading of that passage, was, *"Uh oh! Dumb move!"*

Later, though, I read a devotional in *Our Daily Bread*, about how when the prophet Isaiah prophesied to King Hezekiah that everything he had accumulated was going to be carried off,[4] Hezekiah received Isaiah's word of prophecy graciously, because he thought there would be peace and security in his lifetime.[5] Ordinarily, whenever I would read this biblical account, I would always think to myself, "How dumb and naïve Hezekiah was to reveal all of his treasures to the son of the King of Babylon like that! It was so obvious that those guys were casing the joint!"

But, by that time in my life, God was busy doing some major work in me and my relationship to stuff. So, I got something new from that scripture passage: If I want to unburden myself of the stronghold of all the clutter in my life that needs to go so I can move forward into the freedom God has for me, then I'm going to have to disclose its existence. And not just some of it, but I have to reveal the truth of ALL of it if I hope to get any help carting it off and out of my life!

Then, like Hezekiah, I will claim that the Word of the Lord is good and that there *will* be peace and security in my lifetime![6] And if peace and security come at the cost of disclosing all my "treasures" (aka clutter) in order to ask for and receive help, then so be it.

I've experienced several different times in my life in which it was necessary to enlist the help of others. Usually, these times precede things like a major move, but sometimes they involve something as simple as impending company to my home. I thank God for compassionate sisters-in-Christ who have come to my aid during urgent times of need. Each time felt like a situation in need of a miracle because it would have been physically impossible for me to single-handedly accomplish what needed to be done in the narrow window of time I had to meet my goal.

In fact, I was facing one of those times when I was writing this chapter. I had less than 48 hours to de-junk a large, underutilized room and convert it back into an attractive, welcoming room for receiving guests. It had been a few years since we'd last entertained guests due to a crisis that had turned our world upside down for a while. My husband had a serious, life-threatening accident that rendered him physically disabled for a year. As a by-product of the post-traumatic stress, I was more-or-less emotionally disabled for a while, immediately following the accident. With my husband unable to work, I ended up taking on a couple of part-time jobs, meanwhile letting things "slide" at home.

Hubby has recuperated, and after two years, is finally back to full-time employment. I now have three part-time jobs, in addition to my writing, and consequently do very little on a regular basis to keep up with home tasks and upkeep. We both enjoy our work and have adapted to this new way of living, but family obligation called, so I was forced out of this form of "household hibernation."

My ministry of home hospitality, which had lain dormant for too long, was being called into action. Why? My daughter was going to be visiting from out of state. I confided my conundrum to a trusted friend who was willing to come and work with me to restore some order to this place.

Having someone over to help tidy up a house in such a state can be scary, believe me, but we just have to press forward through the fear. So, cling with me to the truth in God's Word, which tells us this:

> **"The Lord God helps me, so I will not be ashamed.**
> **I will be determined, and I know**
> **I will not be disgraced."**
> —Isaiah 50:7

PRAYER

Forgive me, Lord, for having let the fear of what others might think of me prevent me from asking for help when I need it. I know that You have people in Your Body of believers who can help me in the areas in which I am weak—other women who can help me to get my house in order.

But, Lord, I've been so afraid for anyone to see just how weak I am in this area. My hesitation has been rooted in the fear that my character would be judged based on my poor housekeeping. Father, please protect me from cruel judgment. Help me, Lord, to move beyond this fear and ask for the help I need.

Father, forgive me for my pride in not trusting Your Family to know the truth about my weakness. I am so sorry for allowing my sinful pride to interfere with fulfilling my ministry of hospitality. I rebuke and renounce pride in Jesus' Name! Jesus, I ask you to break pride's hold on me and on my life. Pride has no right to mess with me or my family anymore! I claim the blood of Jesus over me and my home and ask that You would "… let me not be put to shame …" (Ps. 25:2).

Lord, I crave deeper intimacy with You. I now realize that it is time to also risk that kind of intimacy within Your Family. You are faithful, Lord, in leading me out of the bondage of shame, into a "spacious place" of courage, trust, acceptance, and gratitude.[7] Now is the time for me to put my faith in You and be willing to receive Your love, help, and acceptance through the members of Your Body. Even Jesus, in His perfection, functioned within a select group of close friends.

Heavenly Father, give me the wisdom and discernment to know who You would have me reach out to for help. Please direct me to women who will have compassion and understanding, and who won't think less of me because of my struggle with clutter. Holy Spirit, please show me whom You would have me ask for help in this area. Bring to my mind the ones I can call upon for assistance with clearing out the clutter and restoring order to my home. Holy Spirit, show me those individuals within Your Body through whom You want to do a miracle in my home and in my life.

Thank You for putting safe people in my life—those I can trust and turn to for help. And thank You, Lord God, for giving me the determination to move through my fear so that I may complete my decluttering goals. Thank You for helping me, so I will not be ashamed. And thank You for the promise that I will not be disgraced. I pray this in Jesus' Name. Amen.

TAKE ACTION

- Spend some quiet time alone with the Lord. Ask the Holy Spirit to bring to mind the name (or names) of someone God wants to use for His Glory in helping you reach your home-decluttering goals.

- Call that person now and ask for help. If she is able and willing to help, set a date and time for a decluttering session together. If it is within your means, offer to either pay your helper or to exchange services in compensation (perhaps babysitting, cleaning, or some other service arrangement that works out for both of you).

- If your friend is unable to help at this time, ask her if perhaps the Lord has put someone else on her heart who might be able and willing to help. If so, follow up with that other person.

- In either case, once you have set a date and time to get together for a decluttering session, mark it on your calendar. Then begin gathering whatever supplies you will need for the decluttering session.

SUPPLIES LIST

- Garbage bags
- Empty boxes
- Three sheets of paper and a Sharpie pen for making signs ("KEEP," "TOSS," "GIVE AWAY")
- Dust rag
- List of questions (We'll get to those in Chapter 11: In the Valley of Decision.)

(Messy-a.n.i.c. Praise Report: Praise God, ever since we cleared out what used to be my dance studio in preparation for my daughter's visit, I've been able to enjoy using this cozy, inviting space every day now as my new writing studio. God is good.)

Read Chapter 5: **Get More Done by Working Together** for a *Breakthrough in Fellowship!*

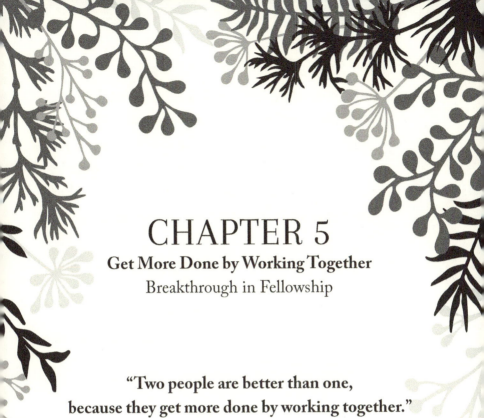

CHAPTER 5
Get More Done by Working Together
Breakthrough in Fellowship

*"Two people are better than one,
because they get more done by working together."*
—Ecclesiastes 4:9

Once you've set an appointment for a decluttering session with the help of a trusted friend, give some thought as to how your helper can best support you in the task at hand. There are a few different ways you can go about making the best use of your helper's time with you:

- If you just need someone to be in the room with you, to help you stay focused on what you're doing, but don't necessarily want or need that person's physical help or input, you could ask your helper to be a "silent accountability partner." As such, her job would be to sit in the room with you while you work, her presence being a reminder that you must stay on task and get as much done as possible while she is there. Your "silent accountability partner" will sit quietly, reading or knitting or occupied in some other quiet task while you are busy decluttering.

- If you want a little more engagement, but still need your accountability partner to work silently, you could have her hand you one thing at a time so you can decide whether to keep, discard, or give the item away.

- If it's a paper decluttering session, you might be making determinations as to which category each paper item belongs to. For example, a friend of mine recently helped me with the dreaded task of decluttering a large tabletop of almost a year's worth of papers and assorted random objects from my very full life as a writer, women's ministry director, worship team musician, children's ministry song and dance teacher, and an officer in a writers' club. Once we identified and established those five categories, I didn't even have to handle every single piece of paper. It was easy for my friend to recognize and make determinations as to which category each paper belonged. Just getting the jumble sorted and put into some kind of order made a sizable dent in the project at hand.

- If you want your helper to assist you in deciding whether to keep or discard objects, you can have her ask you specific questions to facilitate your decision-making process. (We'll go over a list of helpful questions to ask, in Chapter 11: In the Valley of Decision.)

- If the decluttering task you are planning to undertake is just too private or personal for you to share with anyone, but you still need some support and accountability, you could schedule a phone check-in appointment with a friend. This can be very useful and effective if you don't really need the physical help, but you have a hard time forcing yourself to actually start the decluttering session. One time I made an appointment with my decluttering coach, Ceci Garrett (who I mentioned in Chapter 2) to call me at the start time of a major, dreaded decluttering session, to make sure I got started.[1] This helped me immensely, knowing she was going to call me at the beginning of my dreaded decluttering session. The knowledge of her support and commitment to help me meet my goal motivated me to make the necessary preparations. Before our agreed-upon time, I got everything ready that I would need to successfully complete the task. So, when Ceci called me, I was ready to begin. She asked me a few questions pertinent to what I planned to do, and we made an agreement as to how long I would work, as well as an agreement to speak again by phone at the end of the session.

God's Promises:
"I will ask the Father,
and He will give you another Helper
to be with you forever—the Spirit of Truth ..."
—John 14:16

"The Lord is beside you to help you."
—Psalm 110:5a

PRAYER

Thank You, Lord, for Your Word which tells me, **"Two people are better than one, because they get more done by working together"** (Ecclesiastes 4:9). Thank You for bringing my friend, _____, alongside me to work together for Your glory. Thank You, Lord, for having delivered me from that old shame and embarrassment that used to keep me from allowing others to help me.

And thank You, Father, that I am not alone in this, for Your Holy Word declares that You have given another Helper, Your Holy Spirit. Thank You for the assurance that You are beside me to help me (Psalm 110:5a).

Lord, I pray that You will be preparing my heart and mind, and the heart and mind of my friend, _____, before our decluttering session together. Give us both wisdom, Lord, regarding how to best go about the task at hand. God bless my friend, _____, for her willingness to serve You by helping me. In Jesus' Name, I pray. Amen.

TAKE ACTION

1) Choose a specific area to work on. Write it down here:

2) Set a specific goal for that day's session. Write it down here:

3) Decide specifically how you want your friend to help you when she comes over for your decluttering session together. (Refer to the five different options laid out above.) Decide if you want your helper to be a "silent accountability partner" or a more actively involved helper. Write down your decision here:

4) In either case, explain to your friend how she can best help you (whether by remaining a quiet physical presence, or a more hands-on "Clutter Buddy" assistant).

Read Chapter 6: **Don't Fall Off Your Stick**, for a *Breakthrough in Sustenance*.

CHAPTER 6
Don't Fall Off Your Stick
Breakthrough in Sustenance

"But when he becomes hungry, he loses his power.
If he does not drink water, he becomes tired."
—Isaiah 44:12b

I once learned in an outdoor survival training class that if you are only 2% dehydrated, your decision-making ability is impaired by 50%. Decluttering requires making decisions. With that in mind, it's easy to see why it's so important to stay hydrated before and during decluttering sessions.

When my daughter was a young girl, when we were going to be decluttering her room together, she wrote out a "rule" and posted it on the wall in her room. The posted rule sign was a reminder to us that we were required to stop periodically to drink water and have a nutritious snack, to keep our energy up (and our tempers down).

This was a good thing because, if left to my own devices, I tend to lose all track of time and forget to eat or drink anything for hours at a time. That's why I particularly appreciate the verse, Mark 5:43, in which Jesus advised the parents of the 12-year-old girl (who'd just been raised from the dead) to "give the girl something to eat." If we work to the point of depletion, without sustenance, we'll be like that poor girl, needing to be resuscitated. This scripture passage about Jesus raising this girl from the dead reminds us that even when miracles are happening, practical matters still need to be taken care of. After all, we are only human.

> **"But when he becomes hungry, he loses his power. If he does not drink water, he becomes tired."**
> —Isaiah 44:12b

In this verse from the Book of Isaiah, God was reminding the Israelites that, unlike Himself, the workmen were mere humans who required the sustenance of food and water to maintain their strength and power. We are no different. We, too, need to remember to fortify ourselves with nutritious food and water before we undertake any kind of decluttering project. This is for three essential reasons:

- Strength
- Energy
- Decision-making ability

In my husband's Frisian Dutch language, they have a saying to describe being so hungry and depleted that, translated into English, means something to the effect of a starving bird feeling so weak and faint, it's about to fall off the stick upon which it is perched. In essence, you don't want to "fall off your stick."

When I was in Holland last year, I had the opportunity to watch the traditional sport of the Dutch province of Friesland. This Dutch sport of pole vaulting over a canal is called Fierljeppen (pronounced "fear-lee-yeppin.") Translated into English, it means "Far Leaping." The aim of the "Far-Leaping" athletes is to take a running start, grab onto the long pole lodged into the canal bottom at the bank's edge, and climb up the pole as fast as they can so the weight of their body will cause the pole to lean out over the canal. If the pole bends far enough, when they let go of the pole, they'll land on the other side of the canal.

It's an intense sport to watch. And, naturally, a lot of the "Far Leaping" athletes fall off their stick into the water! The goal, of course, is to not fall off your stick! At least not until you've hurdled over your obstacle, which in this case is the canal.

In our case, the hurdle would be overcoming the obstacle of clutter!

From an athletic perspective, it's easy to see how important it is to be properly fueled for such a challenging event requiring such strength, as well as the discernment to know when to hold on and when to let go! It's no different for us in the challenging task of sorting and discarding. We need to be properly fueled—for both strength and discernment, to know when to hold on and when to let go of stuff.

The Lord understands how we need continual refreshment, not only in His Spirit but physically as well. Throughout the New Testament, we can find examples of where Jesus showed concern for the basic needs of His followers. He cares not only about the condition of your soul but also about your physical well-being and your basic need for food and water.

Make it a priority to take care of yourself when you are going to be doing any kind of decluttering work—so you "don't fall off your stick!"

PRAYER

Thank You, Lord, for showing me in Your Word that food and water are necessary for keeping up my strength and energy. And thank You for providing the daily sustenance I need, both physically and spiritually. Thank You for providing me with sufficient nutritious food and clean drinking water for my physical sustenance.

Thank You, most of all, for Your provision for my spiritual sustenance through the soul-nourishing Daily Bread of Your Holy Word and the soul-refreshing Living Water of Your Holy Spirit which seals my salvation.

Give me wisdom, Lord, to not only seek spiritual sustenance in You but to also be a good steward of my body and my energy so that I can glorify You in all that I do. In Jesus' Name. Amen.

TAKE ACTION

1) First of all, if you have not taken the time to eat or hydrate today, stop right now and go get a drink of water. Then grab a handful of nuts or raisins, or a piece of fruit, before moving on to Step 2.

   That's what I just did while I was writing this chapter. I put down my pen, poured myself a cup of coffee with a scoop of grass-fed collagen protein powder, and then grabbed a handful of raisins. (In full disclosure, there may have also been some chocolate involved.)

2) Go outside and find an interesting little stick that looks like a bird's perch. Come back in and set it on your kitchen windowsill or somewhere that it will serve as a visual reminder to keep up your strength so you "don't fall off your stick!"

3) Jot down a few ideas here of quick and easy, nutritious snacks to keep on hand for days when you will be doing decluttering sessions.

4) What's your favorite healthy beverage for staying hydrated? Write it down here, and make sure you have a supply on hand for your next decluttering session.

My favorite healthy beverage for staying hydrated is:

_____.

(I like to make my own refreshing, sugar-free probiotic drink by mixing a tablespoon of raw apple cider vinegar and 1/8 teaspoon of Sweet Leaf stevia into a 16-oz. glass bottle of water. It's helpful to have a few of these already mixed up, in the fridge.)

5) See and hear the awesome real-life testimony of a man who relied on God to keep him from falling off his perch 1,500 feet above the Grand Canyon, armed with nothing but a balance stick and solid faith in Jesus Christ:

   a) If you subscribe to the Discovery Channel, you can watch the full episode of Nik Wallenda's death-defying tightrope walk across the Grand Canyon on *Skywire Live with Nik Wallenda*.[1]

b) If you don't subscribe to the Discovery Channel, there are a couple of short video clips online of Nik Wallenda praising Jesus over and over as he crosses the Grand Canyon on a tightrope.[2,3]

NOTE

On a list of age-appropriate chores for children, you can find the following:
- "Make easy snacks" and "prepare simple snacks" is listed under ages four to five.[4,5]
- "Get their own snacks" is listed under chores for 6-year-old children.[6]
- Children ages six and up can "prepare and serve a snack."[7]

Read Chapter 7: **From Immobilized to Energized** to *kick the lethargy habit!*

CHAPTER 7
From Immobilized to Energized
Breakthrough in Energy

> "As Peter was traveling … he met a
> man … who was paralyzed
> and had not been able to leave his
> bed for … eight years.
> Peter said to him, '… Jesus Christ heals you.
> Stand up and make your bed.'"
> —from Acts 9:32-34

It's depressing enough just being out of commission for eight days with a cold or flu. Can you imagine not being able to get up and move around for eight long years? I can relate to the paralyzed man, Aeneas, whom Peter met in Lydda.[1] My paralysis wasn't a physical disability, though. It was the paralysis of inertia that often accompanies depression, confusion, and the feeling of being overwhelmed.

Have you been there? Not to Lydda. Have you experienced the paralyzing inertia of feeling overwhelmed? Of not being able to force yourself to get up and do what needs to be done? Of not even knowing where to start? I struggled with depression for ten years before Jesus healed me. Then I had to face the facts of my very real struggle with ADD.

With today's neuroscience technology, scientists are now able to photograph the human brain through neuroimaging techniques. This brain imaging provides irrefutable visual proof of how uniquely designed we are. Through brain-imaging technology, it has been discovered and documented that the ADD brain is indeed different from a non-ADD brain.[2,3,4] In recognizing the positive attributes of ADD, though, I don't consider my ADD to be an error on God's part, but rather, evidence of how differently-abled and uniquely gifted He makes each one of us.

> **"God has made us what we are.**
> **In Christ Jesus, God made us to do good works,**
> **which God planned in advance for**
> **us to live our lives doing."**
> —Ephesians 2:10

Like the man in Lydda, have you struggled with an ongoing challenge that's kept you down, preventing you from achieving your goal of creating a tidy, clutter-free home? Whether it's been due to ADD, depression, physical illness, surgery, a major move, heartbreak, grief, or the stress of being a caregiver to a disabled family member or elderly parent, the battle with paralyzing inertia can be very real. But if Jesus can heal a physically paralyzed man in Lydda, He can certainly heal us of the mental/emotional paralysis that prevents us from being able to take positive action steps in the direction we want to go.

> **"Jesus said to her,**
> **'My daughter, your faith has made you well.**
> **Go in peace, and be healed of your trouble.'"**
> **—Mark 5:34, GNT**

24 REASONS

There was a time in my life when I'd experienced a disappointment so devastating that it completely took the wind out of my sails. I became so depressed that I was struggling just to get out of bed each morning and keep going.

One day in particular, it took me about four hours just to force myself to move from my bed to sit near a sunny window in the laundry room. (I knew I needed the sunlight.) That day, in despair, I wrote this to God in my journal:

"The battle I have going on in my spirit is: 'WHY should I get up? WHY should I go forward another day? WHY should I even bother?'"

That day, I came up with not one reason, but *24 Reasons*. I'm sharing these with you here, for whenever you need to encourage yourself. I wrote this in the form of a Hebrew acrostic (in which each line begins with a successive letter of the alphabet.) You can consider it a grown-up form of ABC. I called it:

ABCs of "Why I Should Get Up"
(minus a few letters)

1. A—because I'm ABLE.
2. B—because God has BIGGER and BETTER things in store for me.
3. C—because I CAN.
4. D—because You DELIGHT in me.
5. E—EXERCISE ENERGIZES me.
6. F—because I am FREE in Christ.
7. G—because GOD GOES with me.
8. H—because there is HEALING in HELPING others.
9. I—I am a daughter of the King.

10. J—JESUS loves me.
11. K—KINDRED spirits care about me.
12. L—LIFE is to be LIVED. LIFE abundant.
    LAUGHTER is the best medicine.
13. M—MOVEMENT is MEDICINE for me.
    MOVING to MUSIC is MEDICINAL.
14. N—NOTHING is impossible with God.
15. O—OPTIMISM is not OPTIONAL!
    OPTIMUM living is my ONLY OPTION.
16. P—There is POWER in PRAYER.
    God's PROMISES are true.
17. R—I have a REASON to be here.
18. S—I am SAFE, SANE, and SAVED.
    SUNLIGHT lifts my SPIRITS.
19. V—I am VICTORIOUS in Christ.
20. W—I was made to WORSHIP God.
21. Y—YESTERDAY is gone. YES to today.

PRAYER

Thank You, Lord, for the unique way You've designed and created me to live my life for You. Please help me to be a living example of Your healing power so that people will see and turn to You. Thank You for the lessons I've learned as a result of my times of paralyzing inertia. And thank You that I don't have to live like that anymore.

Heal me, Lord, of immobilizing thoughts and feelings that have impaired my ability to move forward. I praise You, God, that, by Your grace, I am able to stand up and make my bed. Thank You for a continual infilling of fresh, new energy from the Holy Spirit every day, mobilizing me into action. In Jesus' Name. Amen.

TAKE ACTION

- If you haven't already done so today, stand up and make your bed. Or, if you're feeling energetic, change the sheets on your bed. As you do so, think about how great Aeneas must have felt to finally be empowered to get up and make his bed after eight long years!

<u>Memorize Peter's words to Aeneas:</u>
**"Jesus Christ heals you.
Stand up and make your bed."**
—Acts 9:34

- The next time you're having trouble forcing yourself to get up in the morning, let those words of faith break through the lethargy of inactivity. If they empowered Aeneas to stand up and make his bed after eight years, by the grace of God, we can certainly get up and make our bed after eight hours.

- If you are someone who dreads getting out of bed every day, write your own acrostic—*ABCs of "Why I Should Get Up."* Leave the list on your nightstand for those days when you need to remind yourself *"Why I Should Get Up."*

NOTE

On a list of "Age-Appropriate Chores for Children"
- "Make bed" is listed under ages two to five.[5,6,7,8]
- "Make bed every day" is listed under ages six and seven.[9]
- "Make their bed neatly" is listed as a task that children six-to-eight years old should be able to accomplish.[10]

(Messy-a.n.i.c. Praise Report: Since writing this chapter, I've been able to consistently maintain a new daily habit of making my bed. I just think about poor Aeneas, lying in bed those eight long years. If that's not enough, I tell myself that even a two-year-old child can do it. Those little reminders help encourage me to buck up and make my bed every morning. Praise God!)

Read Chapter 8: **Get Dressed**
for a *Breakthrough in Readiness!*

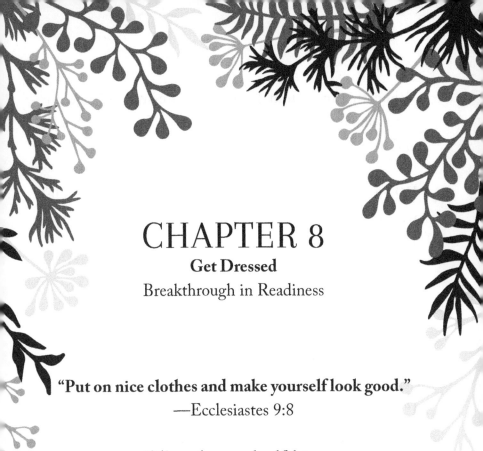

CHAPTER 8
Get Dressed
Breakthrough in Readiness

"Put on nice clothes and make yourself look good."
—Ecclesiastes 9:8

"Then the angel told him,
'Get dressed and put on your sandals.'"
—Acts 12:8a

"Be dressed, ready for service …"
—Luke 12:35a

When Solomon wrote, "Put on nice clothes and make yourself look good," he was exhorting us to enjoy life while we can.

When the angel told Peter, "Get dressed and put on your sandals," he was delivering Peter from the chains and iron gates of the prison.

When Jesus said, "Be dressed, ready for service," He was telling us to be in a state of readiness, waiting for His return.

Each of these words of advice is a good reminder to us in our healing journey as we break out of the chains and iron gates of bondage to clutter, and into a state of readiness to serve the Lord as we await His arrival.

If you have ever struggled with depression or feelings of hopelessness and despair about your situation, you understand how tempting it is to *not* get dressed, to *not* put on your shoes, to *not* make the effort to "make yourself look good." There are a number of reasons you might stay home instead of going to work each day. Whether you work from home, are at home raising babies or young children, or are struggling with health issues or battling depression, it's easy to fall into a routine of staying in your P.J.s and slippers all day. But it's no coincidence that the Word of God specifically gives instructions to get dressed, multiple times. And not *just* get dressed. But to also put on sandals—aka shoes (not house slippers), and to put on *nice* clothes (not ratty, baggy sweats and an old T-shirt). Scripture tells us to "make yourself look good" and to be "ready for service."

As a writer who works from home, I'm often guilty of the P.J.s-all-day routine. I've been known to stay in my P.J.s until I need to leave the house. It's one of the perks of working from home, to be sure. But scripture tells us that more is expected.

For those of us believers who, like Peter, have ever been delivered from any kind of bondage or oppression, or who are awaiting Christ's return, the above biblical instructions are aimed directly at us. We can take these simple words of wisdom to heart as we prepare to declutter our homes.

So, on a day scheduled for a decluttering session, let's be sure to…
- "Get dressed."
- "Put on nice clothes."
- "Make yourself look good."
- "Put on your shoes."
- "Be ready for service."

PRAYER

Thank You, Lord, for Your Holy Word which reminds me of the importance of being "dressed and ready for service." I want to be "dressed and ready for service," Lord. I pray that You would give me the desire to practice this discipline more consistently. In Jesus' Name, I pray. Amen.

TAKE ACTION

1) Lay out your outfit for tomorrow, including what shoes you will wear. Consider making this a daily habit.

2) Write out the passages from Ecclesiastes 9:8 and Luke 12:35a, found at the beginning of this chapter. Jot them down on an index card or large sticky note. Post it where you'll see it when you get up in the morning. Let the words of these verses encourage you to make it a priority to "make yourself look good" every morning so that you'll have a sense of confidence as you begin each day.

NOTE

On a list of age-appropriate chores for children, you will find these:
- "Put shoes on" is listed under chores for two-year-olds.[1]
- "Dress self" is listed under ages four and five.[2]
- "Choose the day's outfit and get dressed" is listed under ages six and seven.[3]
- "Set out clothes the night before" and
- "Can get dressed fully on their own" are listed under chores that children six-to-eight years old can do.[4]

Read Chapter 9: **The Sea of Clutter**
for a *Breakthrough in Hope!*

CHAPTER 9
The Sea of Clutter
Breakthrough in Hope

"He turned the sea into dry land."
—Psalm 66:6a

"He commanded the Red Sea, and it dried up.
He led them through the deep
sea as if it were a desert."
—Psalm 106:9

"But the Israelites walked through
the sea on dry land."
—Exodus 15:19b

"You dried up the sea and the
waters of the deep ocean.
You made the deepest parts of the sea into a road
for your people to cross over and be saved."
—Isaiah 52:10

> **"He speaks to the sea and makes it dry;
> He dries up all the rivers."**
> —Nahum 1:4a

Sometimes when trying to escape that old enemy—clutter—our situation can look hopelessly impossible. When God was leading the Israelites out of captivity in Egypt, their chances of escape looked hopeless. The Pharaoh and his army were rapidly gaining on the Israelites who were faced with the impossible. They were trapped. Trapped between the advancing enemy and the entire Red Sea, with seemingly no way out.[1] But God, Mighty Warrior that He is, *parted* the waters.[2] And …

> **"The Israelites walked through
> the sea on dry ground."**
> —Exodus 15:19a, GNT

How awesome is *that?!*

Whenever the prospect of ever having a clean, clutter-free home looks hopeless, whenever we're feeling trapped between endless demands of daily life and a looming sea of impossible clutter with seemingly no way out, we can call on God for His intervention. Nothing is too big for Him.

> "I am the LORD God of all humanity. Nothing is too hard for me."
> —Jeremiah 32:27, GWT

If you, like me, have been trying to escape the tyranny of clutter for longer than you care to remember, don't be discouraged. The Israelites were afflicted, oppressed, in bondage for *400 years!*[ß] By comparison, our plight diminishes in stature. Whether you've been struggling with clutter for a year, a decade, or a lifetime, it makes no difference.

> "For nothing is impossible with God."
> —Luke 1:37, NLT

Even in the middle of our Sea of Clutter, we can be certain that God is more than able to deliver us and restore our homes back to order.

PRAYER

Lord, I'm so glad that You are a God of miracles! When I feel like I'm drowning in a Sea of Clutter, I know that You can part the waves of chaos and disorder. Lord, just as You made it possible for the people of Israel to walk on dry ground *in the midst of* the sea, I ask You to stretch out Your Mighty Hand over this mess and drive back the Sea of Clutter in my home. Lord, work a miracle, so I can walk through this ocean of clutter.

Deliver me from the enemy whose names are Overwhelment, Confusion, and Disorder. Guide me by Your strength, Lord, into renewed Order and Simplicity. Cast out Excess and Accumulation as I go into the midst of the Sea of Clutter. Deliver me, God, out of this bondage, and into the safety and sanity of a calm, clutter-free home. You are the Lord, my Deliverer. In Jesus' Name. Amen.

TAKE ACTION

Get ready to "cross the Red Sea" of clutter:
- Round up four good-size boxes.
- Boldly label them: "Give Away," "Throw Away," "Put Away," and "Repair or Return."

(Tip: Line the "Throw Away" box with a large plastic trash bag so you will be able to easily remove the contents to discard.)

Read Chapter 10: **Call Me Blessed**, for a *Breakthrough in Faith!*

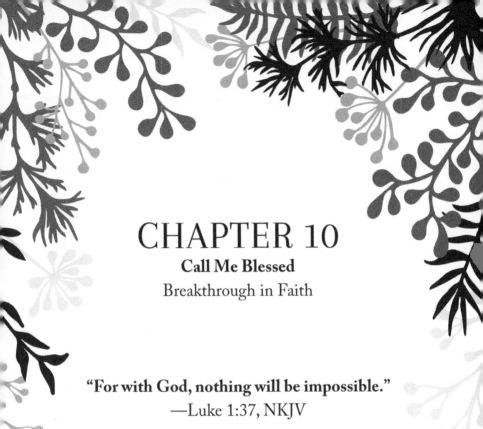

CHAPTER 10
Call Me Blessed
Breakthrough in Faith

"For with God, nothing will be impossible."
—Luke 1:37, NKJV

"Blessed is she who has believed
that the Lord would fulfill His promises to her!"
—Luke 1:45, NIV

As we're believing in God to part that daunting "sea of clutter," we can rest assured that God's miracles neither began nor ended with the famed parting of the Red Sea for the Israelites. A full 620 years earlier, God had performed another particular miracle that speaks to our situation, our struggle with clutter: He took a 90-year-old lady named Sarah, who'd long since given up on the hope of ever having a child of her own, and made her the mother of Isaac,[1] who went on to become the grandfather of the twelve tribes of Israel.[2]

What's important to note here is that the prophecy spoken over Sarah (that she was going to bear a child in her old age) seemed so far-fetched, so absurdly implausible, that Sarah herself laughed aloud when she heard it.[3] But, as we know, God's Word does not come back void. He will always accomplish His purposes.

> "The same thing is true of the words I speak.
> They will not return to Me empty.
> They make the things happen that I want to happen,
> and they succeed in doing what I send them to do."
> —Isaiah 55:11

> **"For no word from God will ever fail."**
> —Luke 1:37, NIV

Sarah wasn't the only old woman in the Bible who conceived and had a child in her old age. Nearly 1,500 years *after* the parting of the Red Sea, another old woman named Elizabeth became pregnant with the one who would grow up to be John the Baptist.[4] Because Elizabeth had waited so long for that miracle of pregnancy, she'd all but given up hope. But when she did indeed become pregnant...

> "Elizabeth said,
> **'Look what the Lord has done for me!**
> **My people were ashamed of me,**
> **but now the Lord has taken away that shame.'"**
> —Luke 1:25

What's more, before Elizabeth's baby was born, an even more unlikely pregnancy occurred to a relative of Elizabeth. An unmarried, virgin girl named Mary became pregnant through Immaculate Conception.[3] The angel Gabriel told Mary she was going to give birth to the Son of God, *and* that her relative Elizabeth was *also* going to have a baby in her old age, saying,

> **"God can do anything!"**
> —Luke 1:37

What do all these nature-defying pregnancies and miracle babies have to do with us and our struggle with clutter? They just go to prove that no matter how implausible our dreams might seem, no matter how long we've been trying with no real results to show for it,

> **"Nothing is impossible for God!"**
> —Luke 1:37, CEV

Even though Sarah truly believed she was past her "Sell By" date, God was still able to perform a miracle in Sarah's life. Likewise, He performed the same miracle in Elizabeth's life. In Elizabeth's culture, the inability to conceive a child had brought her shame because her people thought it was a disgrace for women not to have children.

For us 21st-century Messy-a.n.i.c. Christian women (whether we have children or not), in our culture it is considered disgraceful not to have a tidy house. So, I can celebrate with Elizabeth's triumph when she made this statement:

> "My people were ashamed of me, but now
> **the Lord has taken away that shame."**
> —Luke 1:25b

God is not bound by our human limitations. Even though the home of a Messy-a.n.i.c. Christian woman may grow untidy and packed with clutter, God is still a God of Order. Human cells may age, the eggs in women's ovaries may become old and unviable, but God's Power is ageless and everlasting. His Power is eternally viable. There is no expiration date on the miracles God can do.

So, if the Holy Spirit has planted in your heart a seed of hope that you *can* successfully "give birth" to a tidy and clutter-free home, remember Sarah and the joy she felt when she became pregnant with Isaac, and Elizabeth's joy when she became pregnant with John.

As we anticipate that long-awaited miracle God purposed for us, to be able to give birth to a clutter-free home, let's praise God for the great things He has already done for us!

> "God cares for me, His humble servant.
> From now on, all people will say
> **God has blessed me.**
> **God All-Powerful has done**
> **great things for me,**
> and His Name is Holy."
> —Luke 1:48-49, CEV

PRAYER

I praise You, God! No matter how impossible or overwhelming the task may appear, I believe that it is within Your power, Lord, to deliver me and my home from a pattern of domestic confusion, chaos, and household clutter. Help me, in the midst of the mess, to keep my eyes fixed on You and to stay focused on the great things You have done and are doing in my life (rather than on what *I haven't* done or am *not* doing.) Help me to remember how truly blessed I am.

Also let me remember, Lord, that if You could give an aged, barren woman a child, you can just as easily give me a clean, well-organized, orderly home. Not by my strength or merit, but by *Your* grace and goodness, Lord. Though the task seems overwhelming to me, nothing is impossible for *You*.

Thank You, Lord, for the miraculous blessing of a clean, pleasant, well-organized home. I gratefully receive it now, by faith! In Jesus' Name. Amen.

TAKE ACTION

List five blessings that you are thankful for today.

Five great things God has already done for me:

1.

2.

3.

4.

5.

Memorize Luke 1:37

"For with God nothing will be impossible."
—Luke 1:37, NKJV

… because …

"God can do anything!"
—Luke 1:37

Read Chapter 11: **In the Valley of Decision** for a *Breakthrough in Discernment*.

CHAPTER 11
In the Valley of Decision
Breakthrough in Discernment

> "Multitudes, multitudes in the Land
> of the Valley of Decision!
> For the day of the Lord is near in
> the Valley of Decision!"
> —Joel 3:14a

> "Be strong like a man!
> I will ask you questions, and you must answer me."
> —Job 38:3

Pretty much all clutter is the result of deferred decisions, as in, "I can't decide what to do with this, so I'll just leave it here for now." Unfortunately, the words "for now" are the kiss of death to all good intentions for clutter prevention. Too often, "for now" becomes "forever."

I remember once hearing an actress on a TV talk show, who was promoting her new diet book, talking about how "cream" is just a euphemism for "fat." She suggested that to be more honest about what we are ingesting, we should substitute the word "fat" for the word "cream." So, instead of "ice cream," "cream cheese," "whipped cream," "cream pie," and "cream sauce," we should call it what it is: "ice fat," "fat cheese," "whipped fat," "fat pie," and "fat sauce."

The same could be said about those dangerous words, "this" and "for now." Instead of lying to ourselves by saying, "I'll just put *this* here *for now*," we should tell the truth and admit, "I'll just put *clutter* here *forever*." If keeping clutter in that spot forever is not our intention, we shouldn't lie by telling ourselves, "I'll just put this here for now."

Decluttering requires decision-making. And decision-making requires boundaries and guidelines. When the Lord spoke to Joel about judging the nations, He said, **"Let even the weak person say, 'I am a soldier'"** (Joel 3:10). When arming yourself for the battle against clutter, no matter how weak or inadequate you may feel, tell yourself, *"I am a soldier."* Then attack that enemy—clutter—with boldness.

Just as the Lord's day of judging the multitudes of people is near (Joel 3:14), our day of judging the multitude of clutter is here. This judging process requires us to answer certain questions. After Job had suffered for what must have seemed like an eternity, the Lord told him, **"Be strong like a man! I will ask you questions, and you must answer Me"** (Job 38:3, 40:7). Likewise, although we may have suffered from the affliction of clutter for what seems like an eternity, we, too, must be strong and answer questions. And in the process, we need to be as ruthless as calling all those rich, cream-laden foods what they really are: "ice fat," "fat cheese," "whipped fat," "fat pie," and "fat sauce."

I used to say, "My house is fat!" Decluttering a home is like putting your house on a diet. If your house needs to lose the weight and heaviness of too much clutter, you'll need to be brutally honest in answering certain questions. When you are trying to decide whether to "feed" it another possession, or to eliminate certain things from its "diet," there are a number of questions recommended by various decluttering coaches and organizational consultants. All are valid. Here are 17 of the most common ...

QUESTIONS USED IN THE SORTING AND DISCARDING PROCESS:

Whatever is the item in question, insert the name of that item (verbally) in the blank.

1. Is this _____ beautiful?
2. Is this _____ useful?
3. Does this _____ bring me joy?
4. Do I really need this _____?
5. Do I have room for this _____?
6. Do I have a place for this _____?
7. Do I already have something similar to this _____ that I could use instead?
8. Does this _____ fit?
9. Do I really love this _____?
10. What's the worst thing that could happen if I got rid of this _____? Would it be the end of the world? Would I die?
11. If Jesus were coming here to visit, would I honestly need this _____ to fulfill my ministry of hospitality?
12. Does this _____ reflect my current style and values?
13. Does this _____ support me in achieving my goals?
14. If I saw this _____ in a store today, would I even buy it?

15. Does having this _____ make my life easier or better?
16. Might this _____ be of more service to someone else?
17. If I got rid of this _____ and needed one in the future, could I just rent or borrow one? Or buy another one?

If you answer "No" to any of the first 15 questions (or "Yes" to either of the last two questions), it's a safe bet that you should go ahead and get rid of the item in question.

Then, there's always...

THE MOTHER OF ALL QUESTIONS:

"Does this _____ bring me closer to Jesus?" (Of course, except for the Holy Bible, this question will land most anything else in the "TOSS" or "GIVE AWAY" pile.)

For a free downloadable copy of the above **Questions Used in the Sorting & Discarding Process,** go to: http://bit.ly/MessyanicActionGuide.

PRAYER

Forgive me, Lord, for my sins of procrastination and avoidance that have contributed to the current state of clutter in my home. Lord, Your Word says, **"Let even the weak person say, 'I am a soldier'"** (Joel 3:10). I confess that I am weak and inadequate for the task, but even so, I am a soldier in this battle against clutter.

Thank You, Lord, for Your Holy Spirit guiding me when I am in the Valley of Decision. Lord, thank You for giving me clarity of mind and the strength to answer the questions necessary to make decisions about what to keep and what to discard. Thank You, Lord, for the ability to make wise decisions that will bring me closer to my goal of having a tidy, clutter-free home. In Jesus' Name. Amen.

TAKE ACTION

- With a yellow highlighter, highlight all the above questions that speak the most to you. With a red pen, circle the top three to five of those highlighted questions you think will help you most in your decision-making process.

- Take this book with you to your next decluttering task area; leave the book open to that page, and refer to your main highlighted and circled questions as you go through the sorting and discarding process.

- Alternatively, you could write those top three to five questions on an index card or blank sheet of paper; then take that with you to your next decluttering task area to post up on the wall, where you can refer to it as needed.

- If you need help, enlist the aid of a trusted friend or family member to ask you the questions as you go through each item in your current decluttering project.

- As a soldier in the battle of clutter, it's always wise to put on the full armor of God before going into battle. You can pray the above prayer before every time you begin a sorting-and-discarding session.

OPTIONAL

If you have any military-style or camo print clothing, you could wear your camo cargo pants/leggings/tank top/T-shirt/headband (or whatever camo you have) as an outward symbol to remind yourself that you are "a soldier in the battle against clutter."

Read Chapter 12: **Swept and Put in Order** to kickstart your *Breakthrough in Purification!*

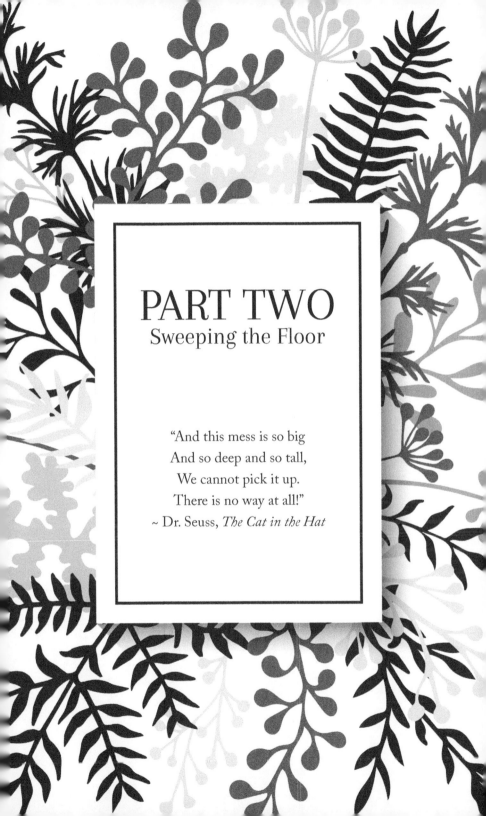

PART TWO
Sweeping the Floor

"And this mess is so big
And so deep and so tall,
We cannot pick it up.
There is no way at all!"
~ Dr. Seuss, *The Cat in the Hat*

CHAPTER 12
Swept and Put in Order
Breakthrough in Purification

> "And when he comes,
> he finds it swept and put in order."
> —Luke 11:25

"Swept and put in order"...This is how I want my home to be when Jesus comes. Until then, in the meantime, every day when my husband comes home from work, and when the kids come home from school, I want them to come home to a house that is "swept and put in order."

I wrote the above paragraph when my kids were teenagers, during a time when God was doing major work in my heart, changing me from the inside out. Luke wrote the parable of the house that was found "swept and put in order," as told to him by Jesus. Only Jesus wasn't really talking about a house. He was talking about a person who is empty inside without the Lord. He could have been talking about you or me, though, or anyone else who's ever tried to fill a vacancy in their heart with something other than God.

When God began healing me of the need to shop and acquire things, He showed me that I had actually been shopping out of loneliness. My husband used to work out of town five to seven days a week, every week, for months on end. Sometimes he didn't even come home on the weekends. I tried not to complain because he was such a diligent worker and a good husband. Although I didn't realize it at the time, I had been using shopping as a distraction from the loneliness I was trying not to feel.

So, in the case of a Messy-a.n.i.c. Christian who is in the habit of shopping and acquiring things to fill the empty ache of sadness, loneliness, grief, or a broken heart, instead of evil spirits coming into the empty house, it's clutter. Too much stuff. What we're really trying to do is stuff our feelings so we won't feel the pain.

Here's the rest of what I wrote that time, about my things being "swept and put in order …"

As the Lord continues to prepare my heart for a season of fasting, He is telling me to prepare for the fast with a season of cleansing and purification: He has shown me that I am to spend 40 days purging the clutter from my home, prior to the fast.

One (of the many) big problems with clutter is that it is not conducive to housecleaning. Stacks and piles of stuff on surfaces (countertops, tables, and floors) make it difficult to sweep and clean. It also makes it nearly impossible for anyone else to help us with our housecleaning. Clearly, housekeeping is no fun when there's excessive clutter in the way everywhere.

If surface clutter is a challenge for you, but you would like to have a home that is "swept and put in order," I hope you will join me in a **40/40 Challenge** of 40 minutes a day, for 40 days, purging the clutter from your home. Let's pray about it....

PRAYER

Dear Jesus, help me to keep focused on You as I go through this upcoming 40/40 Challenge. Give me the will and the stamina to cleanse my home for *You*, Lord, and for *Your* purposes. Thank You, Jesus, for helping me to get (and keep) my house "swept and put in order."

But most importantly, I thank You, Lord, that I do not have to be like that house in the parable about the empty person who is not filled with Your Holy Spirit.[1] Thank You for filling me with your Holy Spirit. In Jesus' Name. Amen.

TAKE ACTION

1) Record the starting date for your 40/40 Challenge here:

   Starting _____, I will devote 40 minutes a day, for 40 days, to decluttering my home in preparation for a season of "fasting."

   Signature:_____
   Date: _____

> For a free downloadable
> **40/40 Challenge Contract with Myself,**
> go to: http://bit.ly/MessyanicActionGuide.

2) Take a sheet of paper and write the numbers 1 through 40 on it. (Alternatively, you can download a free printable 40/40 Chart from the link

below.) Post the chart near where you keep your broom.

Every day, for the next 40 days (or every weekday for the next 8 weeks*), each time you complete your 40-minute decluttering session, either put a checkmark next to that day's number or cross off that day's number. Or, for fun, you could use cute stickers to mark off each day. ;)

*Note: By skipping weekends, your 40/40 Challenge will take 8 weeks (5 days/week x 8 weeks) of decluttering.

For a free downloadable **40/40 Challenge Chart**, go to: http://bit.ly/MessyanicActionGuide.

3) If you haven't already swept and vacuumed your house today, do so now.

4) If your broom is old and worn down, invest in a new broom to use every day during the next 40 days (or 8 weeks, depending on your approach). Then, every time you complete your daily 40-minute decluttering session, sweep the area

where you were working, leaving it "swept and put in order."

NOTE

On a list of age-appropriate chores for children…
- "Sweep floors" is listed under tasks for children ages five to seven.[2]
- "Vacuum individual rooms" is listed under ages six and seven.[3]

A STORY ABOUT PRIORITIES

There's an old Italian folk legend about a woman called La Befana whose hut was always "swept and put in order." La Befana was the extreme opposite of a Messy-a.n.i.c. Christian woman. La Befana was the epitome of a "Martha" persona. To her detriment, La Befana's preoccupation with sweeping and cleaning became her idol. She could not be bothered with following the Lord.

One day, three kings who were in search of the newborn Baby Jesus invited La Befana to join them in going to see the Christ Child. Sadly, La Befana declined, because she was too busy sweeping and cleaning to be bothered. But after the three kings went on their way in pursuit of the newborn King, La Befana regretted her decision. To this day, as the legend goes, every year on the 12th

Day of Christmas, which is Epiphany, La Befana roams the world in search of the Christ Child, leaving a small gift and goodies in the shoes of sleeping children everywhere, in the hope that one of them might be the Christ Child whom she had failed to follow.

Some versions of the legend say that La Befana carries her broom and sweeps the room of every sleeping child she visits, to make it nice and clean for Jesus.

What can we learn from this ancient tale of a misguided soul? Simply this: Jesus does not want us to use our sweeping, tidying, or decluttering efforts as an excuse to keep us from spending time with Him. Rather, He wants us to be on the lookout for opportunities to spend time in His presence, so that we're always ready to receive Him with the invitation, **"Come in, Lord, Please Excuse the Mess!"**

Read Chapter 13: **Captive No More**
for a *Breakthrough in Freedom!*

CHAPTER 13
Captive No More
Breakthrough in Freedom

"I am trapped and I cannot escape."
—Psalm 88:86

"Pull me from the mud, and do not let me sink."
—Psalm 69:14a

"Free me from my prison, and
then I will praise Your Name."
—Psalm 142:7a

"Deliver me from my clutter;
for it is too much for me!
Bring me out of bondage,
that I may give thanks to Thy Name!
Divine Order will surround me;
for Thou wilt deal bountifully with me."
—Prayer adapted from Psalm 142:6-7

> Lord, I look around myself and see nothing but a mess. I clearly can do NOTHING without you! ... So trapped I am in my prison of CLUTTER, CONFUSION, and OVERWHELMENT. How can I serve You, Lord, drowning in this stew of regret, shame, secret anguish? ... Lord, I'm so STUCK! All this stuff around me is like quicksand, pulling me under. I can't move ... Lord, I NEED YOU to SAVE ME from this nightmare! I am a hostage in my own home! HELP ME!!!!!!!
>
> *(Journal entry July 26, 2012)*

Living with too much stuff can feel like a prison sentence. As someone who has struggled with chronic clutter, I can certainly relate to the Psalm that David wrote about feeling trapped and imprisoned by his circumstances. When surrounded by piles of papers and stuff that's out of place, the weight of it can feel heavy and binding, like clay or quicksand.

It's easy to start to believe there is no way out—which is right where the enemy wants us—feeling hopeless. But, like David, we can turn to God. He can free us from any prison of our own making. And when He does, we can praise His Name.

PRAYER

Father God, in Psalm 69:33, Your Word says that You listen to those in need and do not look down on captives. Thank You for listening to me in my need, for I have been a captive of my clutter for too long. I confess, Lord, I am powerless to get myself out of this mess I've made of my physical environment. I am trapped by clutter; I cannot escape by my own power.

Pull me from the mud of confusion and disorder. Deliver me from all the clutter that has been holding me hostage. Deliver me from the debilitating bondage of clutter and disorder in my life, from this day forward. I ask You to give me FREEDOM for the rest of my life! To me, it seems like a big, overwhelming thing, God, but to *You*, it's a cinch. So, I give it all to *You*, God, to conquer it *for* me. You've got a plan. You know exactly the best way for this miracle to happen.

Thank You, Lord, for breaking the chains that had me bound. Deliver me, Lord, from the prison of my own making, "and then I will praise Your Name." In Jesus' Name, I pray. Amen.

TAKE ACTION

1) Read the miraculous account (in Acts 16:23-26) of how God delivered Paul and Silas from captivity when they were trapped in prison.

2) Listen to "Chain Breaker," by Zach Williams. (You can find the Official Lyric Video on YouTube.) Crank up the volume and sing along with feeling!

3) Write out Psalm 111:9a and post it in a prominent place where you will see it and read it daily:

>**"He sets His people free."**
>—Psalm 111:9a

Every time you read this verse, *thank God for setting you free from the bondage of clutter!*

Read Chapter 14: **Defeating the Enemy**
for a victorious *spiritual breakthrough!*

CHAPTER 14
Defeating the Enemy
Breakthrough in Victory

"I am in trouble. Hurry to help me!
Come near and save me;
rescue me from my enemies."
—Psalm 69:17b-18

"Help us fight the enemy.
Human help is useless, but
we can win with God's help.
He will defeat our enemies."
—Psalm 108:12-13

In the spiritual realm, an ongoing battle with clutter isn't really about the stuff. Persistent, chronic clutter and disorganization can become a spiritual stronghold, giving a foothold to the enemy. When clutter has become a spiritual stronghold, if we are to enjoy real victory in the physical realm, we must first deal with it in the spiritual realm. Like Paul told the church in Ephesus:

> **"Our fight is not against people on earth but rulers and authorities and the powers of this world's darkness, against the spiritual powers of evil in the heavenly world."**
> —Ephesians 6:12

The stuff clutter is made of is neutral. Physical matter is neither good nor bad. It's the lies from the enemy, which attack our self-worth, that are evil. The Enemy knows our Achilles' heel—our weak spot—and attacks us in that place where we already feel inadequate, defective, and defeated.

When going into battle, we must know who the enemy is. In the ongoing battle with persistent, chronic clutter and disorganization, the enemy has many names:

Clutter
Chaos
Confusion
Disorder
Disorganization
Indecision
Overwhelmment

Lethargy
Inertia
Mental/Emotional Paralysis
Depression
Shame
Humiliation
Embarrassment
Pride
Perfectionism
Procrastination
Fear
Anxiety
Guilt
Remorse
Regret
Grief
Anguish
Fatigue
Exhaustion
Avoidance

We are forearmed with the knowledge that the battle is already won; thus, we fight against the attacks of the enemy with the ferocity of our full confidence in God to give us victory. New Zealand Pastor Tak Bhana, of Church Unlimited, tells us, *"We don't have to defeat the enemy; Jesus has already done that. What we need to do is use our God-given authority and enforce the victory."*[1]

> "And He said to them,
> '...Behold, I give you authority to trample on...,
> and over all the power of the enemy,
> and nothing shall by any means hurt you.'"
> —from Luke 10:18-19

To enforce the victory, we prepare for battle by putting on the full armor of God.[2] To crush the lies of the enemy, we gird ourselves with the Belt of Truth and wield the Sword of the Spirit, which is the Word of God. We renounce and rebuke every lie as we proclaim the truth found in God's Word.

In the past, we may have felt defeated by our nemesis, clutter, "**… but we can win with God's help. He will defeat our enemies**" (Psalm 108:13).

> "I will call to the Lord, Who is worthy of praise,
> and I will be saved from my enemies."
> —2 Samuel 22:4

> "My God loves me, and He goes in front of me.
> He will help me defeat my enemies."
> —Psalm 59:10

> "God gives me victory over my enemies."
> —Psalm 18:47a

PRAYER

Like David prayed in the Psalms,[3] I admit, Lord, **"I am in trouble. Hurry to help me! Come near and save me; rescue me from my enemies"**—Clutter, Chaos, and Confusion.

Thank You, God, for loving me and going in front of me to defeat the enemy. Thank You for giving me victory over Clutter, Chaos, and Confusion, and all of their evil counterparts.

Forgive me, Lord, for having believed the lies of the enemy in thinking that I could never overcome Clutter and Disorganization. Forgive me for forgetting that with You, Lord, all things are possible.[4]

You've already defeated the enemy by Your death and resurrection. Thank You for saving me from eternal hell and damnation by Your death on the cross. I praise You, God, for wiping out my enemies, Clutter, Chaos, Disorder, Confusion, Indecision, and Overwhelmment *now* in the Name of Jesus, once and for all! And thank You for saving me from the evil powers of darkness that would seek to destroy me, were it not for You going in front of me, defeating my enemies.

I thank You and praise You that in a very short time, this will be but a distant memory; I have full confidence that I will soon be able to testify how *You delivered me* from the oppressor that sought to hold me back from experiencing the fullness of life with You, Lord! Thank

You, Lord Jesus, that because You died on the cross for my sins, I no longer have to live in the dungeon of shame and humiliation. I am free in Christ! Amen. In Jesus' Name! Hallelujah!

TAKE ACTION

1) Read the 27 names of the enemy listed in this chapter. With a yellow highlighter, highlight all the names of the enemy that you've felt most tormented by. With a red pen, circle the main three to five enemies that you most want to defeat.

2) Take a blank sheet of paper and fold it vertically into three columns. **In the column on the left, list those names of the enemy that you have felt personally attacked by.**

3) **In the center column, write the lie associated with that enemy.** For example, the lie of Fear/Shame/Embarrassment that says, "I'm too ashamed of my house to let anyone in to help me because I'm afraid they'll think less of me."

4) Then, **in the column on the right, write what God says about it.** For example, "Don't be afraid, because you will not be ashamed. Don't be embar-

rassed, because you will not be disgraced. You will forget the shame you felt earlier" (Isaiah 54:4a).

5) Do this with every "enemy" listed in your column on the left until you have proclaimed God's Truth over each lie of the enemy. * Then, cross out the lies in the middle column.

6) Ask Jesus to bind each one of those enemies and deliver you from their oppression. Thank Him for giving you victory over your enemies.

7) With scissors, **cut off the right-side column of scripture verses which proclaim God's Truth.** Discard the other side of the paper; **and post the scripture verses in a prominent place** where you will see them every day and be reminded of God's Truth.

*More Examples of God's Truth Over Lies from the Enemy:

Names of the enemy	Lies from the enemy	God's Truth
CONFUSION & OVERWHELMMENT	"I feel so confused and overwhelmed! I don't know where to start."	"God is not a god of confusion but a God of Peace" (1 Cor. 14:33). "Nothing will hold you back; you will not be overwhelmed" (Prov. 4:12).
GUILT	"I feel so guilty for letting things pile up, and for not managing better."	"There is now no condemnation for those who are in Christ Jesus" (Rom. 8:1).
FATIGUE & EXHAUSTION	"I don't have the energy to face my clutter; I'm always too tired to deal with it."	"He gives strength to those who are tired & more power to those who are weak" (Isa. 40:29).

For a free downloadable list of **Scripture Verses of God's Truth for Rebuking the Enemy,** go to: http://bit.ly/MessyanicActionGuide.

Read Chapter 15: **When Clutter Becomes a Spiritual Battle,** for a *Breakthrough in Strength.*

CHAPTER 15
When Clutter Becomes a Spiritual Battle
Breakthrough in Strength

"An enemy might defeat one person,
but two people together can defend themselves;
a rope that is woven of three strings is hard to break."
—Ecclesiastes 4:12

"Also, I tell you that if two of you on earth
agree about something and pray for it,
it will be done for you by My Father in
heaven. This is true because if two or three
people come together in My name,
I am there with them."
—Matthew 18:19-20

By now, you may have already enlisted the help of a trusted friend to serve in some way as an accountability partner/helper/support person for the actual physical process of decluttering. But if you're starting to realize that there may be a spiritual battle around your chronic clutter, it's time to engage in spiritual warfare.

A spiritual battle calls for spiritual warfare. By that, I mean *prayer* support.

If dealing with chronic clutter has been a persistent, ongoing battle for you, no matter how many books you read about how to conquer it, no matter how many workshops or courses you've taken, and no matter how many support groups you join, then it's very likely that clutter has become a spiritual battle for you. A battle in which the enemy has been using your challenge with physical clutter to attack your mind. The way we fight back in a spiritual battle is through prayer and the Word of God, with the help of the Army of God: brothers and sisters in Christ.

So far, we've been praying together up to this point. Now it's time to get one or two other prayer partners involved. Because when we're doing something positive to glorify the Lord, like restoring order and spaciousness to our homes, the enemy is bound to lash out. Nehemiah experienced this when he was helping the people of Jerusalem rebuild the city wall. He was told, **"Everywhere you turn, the enemy will attack us."**[1] His response was to tell them,

> "Don't be afraid of them.
> Remember the Lord ... is great and powerful.
> Fight for ... your homes."
> —from Nehemiah 4:14

From then on, Nehemiah made sure that the people were armed for battle at all times.[2] There are a few key ways we can adopt Nehemiah's spiritual battle plan of defense as we "fight for our homes":

1) We arm ourselves for battle by putting on the full armor of God so we can fight against the devil's evil tricks. We put on God's full armor—with the Belt of Truth, the Breastplate of Righteousness, the Shoes of the Good News of Peace, the Shield of Faith, the Helmet of Salvation, and the Sword of the Spirit, which is the Word of God (See Ephesians 6:11-17).

2) Pray ... at all times with all kinds of prayers, asking for everything you need.[3] Nehemiah knew their enemies were trying to scare them, thinking they would get too weak to work, and that the project would not be finished. So, his prayer was,

> "God, make me strong."
> —Nehemiah 6:9

3) Enlist the help of one or two prayer partners to pray with you before "going into battle" to conquer clutter and "rebuild" an orderly home.

4) Ask your Bible Study group and/or church Prayer Chain to be praying for you as you work through the process of decluttering your home. Ask them to pray for strength for you to finish the task.

God's Promise:
**"So don't worry, because I am with you.
Don't be afraid, because I am your God.
I will make you strong and will help you;
I will support you with My right hand that saves you."**
—Isaiah 41:10

PRAYER

Lord, help me to rebuild order into my home. Like Nehemiah, I pray, **"God, make me strong."**[4] **"Give me, Your servant, success today."**[5] Please give me the stamina and fortitude—physically, mentally, and emotionally—to have a successful, productive day. In Jesus' Name, I pray. Thank You and amen.

TAKE ACTION

1) Read Ephesians 6:11-17. Write out the components of the full armor of God and post it where you'll see it when you're getting dressed every morning.

2) Write here the names of one or two people you can ask to be prayer partners with you, to pray with you before you "go into battle" decluttering your home.

   These are people I can ask to be prayer partners with me:

3) Have a conversation with each of them, requesting their prayer warfare in the spiritual battle against clutter. You might even share with them the list of scripture verses you compiled in the previous chapter (Chapter 14: "Defeating the Enemy") and ask them to pray those scripture verses, claiming God's Truth for you. Make a plan to call them for prayer before your next decluttering session.

4) If your church has a Prayer Team or Prayer Chain, fill out a prayer request card or make a phone call to be put on the prayer chain. Ask for protection from the enemy and for strength to finish the task of decluttering and restoring order to your home.

Read Chapter 16: **Emotional Ties that Bind Us to Clutter** to find out *why we get stuck* and *how to let go*.

CHAPTER 16
Emotional Ties that Bind Us to Clutter
Breakthrough in Release

"Your heart will be where your treasure is."
—Luke 12:34; Matthew 6:21

"Why is it so hard to let go of things?!?" asked a member of one of my online support groups in a post on the Facebook page this morning.

Are you wondering the same thing?

In *Downsizing the Family Home*, author Marni Jameson quotes grief expert, Russell Friedman, in reference to our universal tendency to want to avoid sorting and discarding possessions.

Friedman, who is Executive Director of the Grief Recovery Institute and co-author of *The Grief Recovery*

Handbook and *Moving On*, said, "Many people don't make changes at home they need to make because they're afraid of the feelings they will have."[1] He added, "People avoid moving and making changes at home ... because they're afraid of being sad ..."[2] and, "Too many people stay stuck in an unrewarding place because they're afraid of their feelings."[3]

No wonder we can get stuck! Sometimes, even after asking ourselves all the right questions to help with our decision-making process (See Chapter 11: "In the Valley of Decision"), we might experience an unreasonable or irrational resistance toward letting go of a particular item or group of items. When this happens, it's time to ask the Holy Spirit to show us what is the real underlying reason we cannot bring ourselves to part with an item we don't need or use anymore.

As I stated in Chapter 14, "Defeating the Enemy," the stuff that clutter is made of is neutral. A book or a dish or garment is neither good nor bad. It's just an object. But when we find ourselves unable to let go, it's usually because there is an emotional attachment associated with that item.

It's very common to mistakenly believe that getting rid of an object associated with another person would be the same as getting rid of the person. Of course, intellectually, we know that's nonsense. I experienced a similar reluctance once when I was thinning out my coat closet in preparation for a move to a slightly warmer climate. I had a beautiful, turmeric-gold, wool swing coat that I no longer wore. Although there was nothing wrong with the garment, it was no longer in style; it had also been years since I'd worn it.

At the time, I was participating in a *Buried in Treasures* workshop series facilitated by clutter hoarding coach, Ceci Garrett, founder of Lightening the Load ministry.[4,5] Our homework assignment was to do a cognitive behavior experiment if we came across a particular item that, without any rational reason or justification, we were unable to part with. The experiment was to place the item in the middle of the room and pay attention to any feelings that came up as we thought about getting rid of the object in question. This goes along with Jameson's and Friedman's recommendation to "Feel the feeling."[6]

Only someone who has struggled with clutter and the challenging work of discarding things could understand how scary and difficult it might be to do such an experiment. But we have the Lord to help us.

> **"So don't worry, because I am with you.
> Don't be afraid, because I am your God."**
> — Isaiah 41:10a

When I did this experiment with my coat, instead of resisting the prospect of getting rid of the coat, I allowed myself to feel whatever emotions would come up if I were to let the coat go. To my surprise, grief rose up in me and I bawled my eyes out. After a deeply cathartic crying session, I understood what had kept me stuck and unable to part with this neutral, inanimate object. I remembered that it was the coat I'd worn after my second child was born. I recalled wearing my baby in a "Snuggli" while wearing that coat. I would wrap the roomy swing coat around my baby to keep him warm.

So, it wasn't the potential loss of the coat I was grieving. It was the passing of my child's infancy and childhood that I mourned. My son had grown up, graduated from high school, and recently moved into his own apartment. I had a classic case of empty nest blues. My subconscious mind apparently thought that, by holding onto that coat, I could avoid feeling the sadness and loss of his infancy and childhood. The loss was doubly hard, too, because his father had passed away a year or so before that. Although we'd been divorced for quite some time, there was still repressed grief from that tragic and unexpected loss.

Through this experience, I learned that I would survive even if I got rid of the coat. By allowing myself to feel the buried feelings associated with the object (in this case, a coat), the item no longer had a hold on me. I was able to easily let go of it; in fact, I have never once looked back, wishing I still had it. The tie to the item that had kept me in bondage—from being able to make a healthy, functional decision to get rid of an object I no longer used or needed—was no longer there.

And, almost as a confirmation of having done the right thing by releasing that coat, after that, my relationship with my son was even more rewarding. I was able to fully appreciate the young man he'd grown to be, rather than remain stuck grieving the loss of the baby and child he no longer was. As a result, my heart was rightly placed with my son, rather than on an object associated with my son.

> **"Your heart will be where your treasure is."**
> Matthew 6:20; Luke 12:34

PRAYER

Thank You, Lord, for sending Your Helper, the Holy Spirit, to assist me when the going gets rough in this emotionally trying process of letting go and releasing the clutter in my life. Thank You, Lord, that I need not fear, for You are with me every step of the way. Holy Spirit, I ask that You reveal to me the underlying reasons I can't bring myself to part with certain items I no longer use or need. Heavenly Father, in the Name of Jesus, I ask You to break off any emotional ties that may have kept me bound up, attached to my clutter. In Jesus' Name. Amen.

TAKE ACTION

Ask the Holy Spirit to reveal to you any unnecessary object(s) or group of objects in your home that have emotional ties attached to them which make it difficult to let go and release them. Write down what comes to mind here:

As an experiment, place that difficult-to-release item in the middle of the room. Allow yourself to feel whatever feelings come up for you when you think about letting go of that item. Just sit with the feeling, knowing that it's only a feeling, and that you are in no danger. When you have fully experienced the whole gamut of whatever feelings that item brought up for you, write about it here:

After doing this experiment, if you feel comfortable to do so, discard the item in question.

Repeat this Action Step whenever you feel stuck and unable to let go of something you know you should get rid of.

Read Chapter 17: **"Fuh Gedda Bow Dit"**
to learn why forgetfulness is a *good* thing.

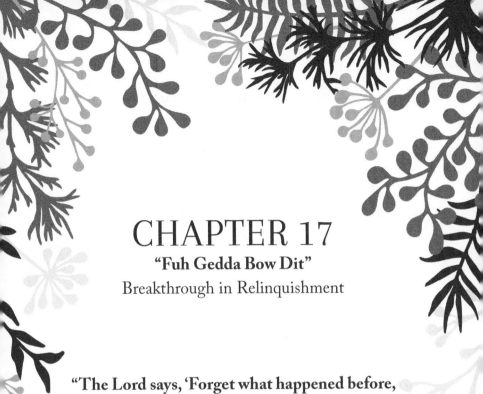

CHAPTER 17
"Fuh Gedda Bow Dit"
Breakthrough in Relinquishment

"The Lord says, 'Forget what happened before, and do not think about the past.'"
—Isaiah 43:18

There was a great scene in an old gangster movie in which an undercover cop who'd infiltrated an organized crime family was explaining to his law enforcement colleagues the multipurpose use of the gangsters' phrase, "Forget about it." (Pronounced, "Fuh gedda bow dit.")

Although it's fun to say **"Fuh gedda bow dit,"** actually doing that isn't so easy. This is why we might tend to avoid decluttering work. Because, just like we can have emotional attachments to our clutter, we can also have a lot of memories attached to our stuff.

I'm not talking about ordinary, nostalgic, fond memories. Sorting through stuff that brings up happy memories can bring a smile to your face. But it can be difficult when we come across objects that remind us of our failures, shortcomings, and mistakes we've made in the past. To avoid being confronted with these kinds of less-than-happy memories, it's tempting to avoid putting time and energy into the sorting process necessary for successful decluttering.

A common memory that might be triggered by certain objects is the recollection of having made a poor decision. For example, you might have a garment or pair of shoes you bought but have never worn. Every time you see that item, you might feel a twinge of guilt for having wasted money on something that you didn't need and that is of no use to you. But you can't bring yourself to get rid of it, because you paid good money for it. Besides, if you keep it, maybe you'll use it someday. Also, if you get rid of it, that would be admitting you made a mistake by buying that thing in the first place.

This kind of thinking can trap us into keeping stuff we simply need to let go of. This applies to not only physical clutter but also the mental clutter of remembering every wrong thing we've ever said or done.

I recently posted a quote on the page of a Facebook group that centers on the topic of decluttering.[1] The quote said, "Don't cling to a mistake just because you spent a lot of time making it." I posted a comment with it, saying, "Likewise, don't cling to a mistake just because you spent a lot of money on it."

A professional bookkeeper/accountant in the group then commented, "In accounting, we call that a 'spent cost' and it shouldn't be used in determining the future!"

Past failures, mistakes, or poor decisions are "spent costs." In *Downsizing the Family Home*, Mark Brunetz, co-author of *Take the U out of Clutter*, says, "Why hang onto something that reminds you of something that didn't work?"[2] What's done is done. The time and/or money wasted on past mistakes are "spent costs." Holding onto those items will not redeem the time or money wasted on these regretted mistakes from our past.

If there was anyone who had things in his past he regretted, it was the apostle Paul (who also went by Saul). Before God got a hold of him, Saul was hell-bent on persecuting Christians. But after God got Saul's attention, this apostle spent the rest of his life serving Christ by spreading the Good News about Jesus.

If he'd let himself get hung up on his past, Paul would have never been able to live out the life of service God had planned for him. Instead of looking backward, beating himself up over things he couldn't change, Paul stayed forward focused, aimed at carrying out his God-given mission to bring the Good News to the Gentile world.

He shared with his brothers and sisters in Christ about his **"Fuh Gedda Bow Dit"** discipline in keeping a forward-focused momentum in his spiritual walk. Paul wrote this to the Christians in Philippi:

> **"Brothers and sisters,**
> **I know that I have not yet reached that goal,**
> **but there is one thing I always do.**
> **Forgetting the past and**
> **straining toward what is ahead,**
> **I keep trying to reach the goal."**
> —Philippians 3:13-14a

In the previous verse (v.12) Paul admitted, **"I have not reached that goal, but I continue trying to reach it and to make it mine."** And the way he did that was by forgetting what happened before and not thinking about the past (as God commanded in Isaiah 43:18.) Paul instead chose to constantly remember his goal and what he was working towards, keeping focused straight ahead, with his eye always on the desired outcome.

That, my friend, needs to be our attitude as well. Whatever errors we may have made yesterday or 5,000 yesterdays ago, God advises us to "**Fuh gedda bow dit.**"

> "**The Lord says,**
> '**Forget what happened before,**
> **and do not think about the past.**
> **Look at the new thing I am going to do.**
> **It is already happening. Don't you see it?**'"
> —Isaiah 43:18-19a

PRAYER

Thank You, Lord, for Your Word that reminds me to forget what happened before, and to not think about the past. I know that Your Word says You have taken my mistakes away from me "as far as the east is from the west" (Psalm 103:12). Help me, Lord, to let go of them as well. Help me instead to hold onto my vision of the clutter-free life You have for me.

Keep my heart, mind, and eyes focused on You and why You want me to have a clutter-free home—so I can better serve You and fulfill my ministry of hospitality, Lord. In Jesus' Name, I pray. Amen.

TAKE ACTION

- Ask the Holy Spirit to bring to your awareness anything among your belongings that is a "spent cost." Either chuck it into the trash, toss it into a giveaway bag, or set it out at the curb with a big "FREE" sign—because that's what you'll be without it: **FREE**. No regrets. Don't look back. So *what* if you paid good money for it?! **Fuh gedda bow dit!**

Repeat this Action Step as many times as necessary until you've discarded any and all "spent cost" items that may have been lurking around your house serving as reminders of regrets about past mistakes.

Write down here whatever "spent cost" items you were able to free yourself from:

Read Chapter 18: **From Avoidance to Forgiveness** to learn about the healing power of *Compassion*.

CHAPTER 18
From Avoidance to Forgiveness
Breakthrough in Compassion

"There is therefore now no condemnation for those who are in Christ Jesus."
—Romans 8:1, RSV

It took me nearly a year of deep introspective work, of the Lord cultivating my heart, to be able to fully accept the spiritual truth in that famous statement issued by the apostle Paul when he wrote to the Christians in Rome: **"There is therefore now no condemnation for those who are in Christ Jesus"** (Romans 8:1, RSV).

That can be a tough one to believe if we happen to be avoiding buried feelings—feelings we can't even access, let alone acknowledge. But the Lord seriously began the business of doing a work in my heart when, taking a leap of faith, I stepped out of my comfort zone to participate in a "Celebrate Recovery" Step Study. Although I wasn't exactly clear about what I was supposed to be "working on" my first time through the study, I just knew that I really wanted to "celebrate recovery" among fellow believers. My big "Aha!" moment came near the end of the study when I had the realization that my "issue," at that time, was AVOIDANCE.

Nevertheless, it was that first CR Bible Study that began to prepare my heart for what lay ahead. Following that first Step Study, the Lord led me to the next thing He had in store for my spiritual healing journey: a workshop series led by professional clutter coach and founder of *Lightening the Load* ministry, Ceci Garrett.[1] The 15-week workshop series was based on the book, *Buried in Treasures: Help for Compulsive Acquiring, Saving, and Hoarding*.[2] In that "Buried in Treasures" workshop series, I was first introduced to the cognitive behavior experiment which I described in Chapter 16, "Emotional Ties That Bind Us to Clutter."

> **"What are you avoiding?"**
> —Mark Brunetz[3]

[Side note about **Avoidance**: It was in the course of the "Buried in Treasures" workshop series when I realized that, unbeknownst to us, sometimes our clutter is tied to painful feelings. Ironically, sometimes clutter is really a mask for unrecognized pain hiding under and behind all of our excess stuff, all of our "treasures," causing us yet more pain. But the authors of that book cleverly chose the word "Treasures" because who would ever sign up for a class called "Buried in Pain"?!]

It was also during the "Buried in Treasures" workshop series that I finally came to terms with the fact that I needed spiritual healing for a life-changing choice I'd made several years before that. It was something I'd tucked away so I wouldn't have to think about it. I wanted to "fuh gedda bow dit."

In our culture, we often hear the phrase, "forgive and forget." To which, someone will usually quip, "I can forgive, but I'll *never forget!*" Sometimes, though, the reverse is true. Sometimes we aren't able to forgive, but we will bury something so that we can forget about it. This had happened to me, and the Holy Spirit brought it to my awareness as a result of the cognitive behavior experiment that I described in chapter 14.

Not long before that, I had been working as an Activities Assistant in a long-term-care, assisted-living facility. With dementia and Alzheimer's patients, it was common for residents to enjoy having or holding a baby doll. Especially a lifelike one. So, I bought a lifelike baby doll that giggled just like a real baby. I dressed it in a real baby diaper and real baby clothes and would take it to work with me so the residents could take turns "holding the baby" during some of our group activities. After I left that line of work and no longer had a use for the doll, I kept it—even though I had never been a girl who played with dolls when I was growing up.

In preparation for a major cross-country move, relocating to another state, I participated in the "Buried in Treasures" workshop series. I needed help in making some changes in my relationship with things, so I could let go of a lot of stuff—to be able to effectively pack and move. But for some unknown, irrational reason, I couldn't let go of that baby doll. My daughter even thought it was weird that I still had it, but I just couldn't bring myself to get rid of it.

However, the Holy Spirit used that simple object, a lifelike doll, to bring to my awareness something that I needed the Lord to heal in me. That sweet little baby doll that I couldn't let go of made me realize that I needed to seek spiritual help and healing for an abortion I'd had secretly, several years before I was saved.

After completing the "Buried in Treasures" workshop series, which helped me to get to the core of some of the things I'd been AVOIDING, I was ready for God to do some more healing work in me. Next, I signed up for an eight-week "Path of Life" Bible study for post-abortive women in the city where I lived.

Although emotionally challenging, the intensive study proved to be a very healing experience, which I would highly recommend for anyone who's had an abortion. The healing that I experienced as a result of going through that "Path of Life" Bible study enabled me to finally forgive myself for the "unforgivable" choice I'd made to terminate a pregnancy. (My former New Age indoctrination had had me falsely believing that the soul doesn't enter the body until the moment of birth; that was how I had justified my actions. Now I know better.)

There was a certain part of the study in which we were looking at the story of how King David committed adultery with Bathsheba, the wife of one of David's soldiers. Oddly enough, in my previous ten years of daily Bible study, I'd never really recognized myself in that biblical account of infidelity. But during the "Path of Life" study, the Holy Spirit removed the scales from my eyes; for the first time, I understood Bathsheba. What's more, I could see myself in Bathsheba. And for the first time, I saw her through eyes of compassion.

The Holy Spirit gently revealed to me how such a transgression could happen. It became so clear to me: Bathsheba was *lonely*. Her husband was always gone, away, at work. And, for the first time, God allowed me to see my earlier self through eyes of compassion instead of condemnation. I, too, had been so lonely, touch-starved, and vulnerable to sins of the flesh. It did not justify or excuse my erroneous actions; but, looking back, with the discernment of the Holy Spirit, I could see how truly needy I'd been … and how it was that I'd so easily slipped and given in to temptation.

Although I still hate and regret what I did as a result of that, I do not hate myself. Because God has shown me His compassion, I have received the truth of Romans 8:1.

> **"There is therefore now no condemnation for those who are in Christ Jesus."**
> —Romans 8:1, RSV

After working through all that, by the grace of God, I was able to finally forgive myself, and had no trouble releasing the doll. That inanimate little baby doll had served as a messenger to help me seek and obtain the healing I'd needed. Praise the Lord.

Perhaps my story here brings something to mind for you of an event or something in your own life that you've managed to "fuh gedda bow dit," but haven't been able to forgive yourself for. Let's pray about it…

PRAYER

Lord, thank You for loving me unconditionally, in spite of the times I've succumbed to temptation. I am so grateful, Jesus, to be in You and to have Your Holy Spirit in me. If there's anything in me or in my past that I've buried or tried to forget about, for which I need to forgive myself, I ask You to show me now. Even though I know that you have taken my mistakes from me "as far as the east is from the west,"[4] I confess that I haven't always been so forgiving of myself. Lord, if there is anything stopping me from forgiving myself, I ask that You break off and bind that spirit of condemnation right now, in the Name of Jesus. Amen.

TAKE ACTION

<u>Materials needed:</u> A piece of paper, a pencil, a black permanent marker, an eraser, and either a woodstove, fireplace, BBQ grill, or paper shredder.

1) If the Holy Spirit has brought to your awareness something you need to forgive yourself for, write it down in pencil on a piece of paper.

2) Confess to God your previous reluctance to forgive yourself for that offense. Ask Him to give you a heart of compassion towards yourself regarding the matter. Thank Him for erasing and forgetting your sins, for He says,

"I am the One who erases all your sins for My sake; I will not remember your sins."
—Isaiah 43:25

3) Using a permanent marker, write, "I FORGIVE MYSELF" over what you'd written in pencil. When the ink is dry, take an eraser and erase what you'd written in pencil.

4) Dispose of the paper by burning it in a woodstove, fireplace, or BBQ grill; or simply shred it in a paper shredder.

NOTE

According to information provided on Spokane, Washington's Life Services website, "By age 45, a third of all women will have had at least one abortion. 65% of women who choose abortion self-identify as Christian. In fact, one in three people in and out of the church are post-abortive."[5]

(For a list of post-abortion healing and recovery resources, see More Resources for Spiritual Healing & Recovery in the back of this book.)

Read Chapter 19: **Can't Take It with You**
for a *Breakthrough in Perspective!*

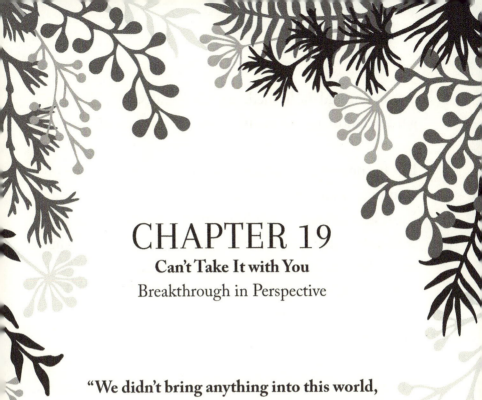

CHAPTER 19
Can't Take It with You
Breakthrough in Perspective

*"We didn't bring anything into this world,
and we won't take anything with us when we leave."*
—1 Timothy 6:7, CEV

"You CAN take it with you" had become my defiant mantra. I spent considerable time and energy trying to prove it, during a year-long period of pre-packing and preparing for a cross-country move from the home where I'd raised my children.

I was most successful in this from a horticultural standpoint. With the help of my husband, I dug up, transported across two states, passed agricultural inspections at state borders, and transplanted a veritable nursery of trees and shrubs—most of which are still thriving to this day in the old-fashioned, arts-and-crafts style, cottage garden landscape we created here at our present home.

But in spite of my successful landscaping, and in spite of countless hours of help from a couple of friends—first, Lois, who helped sort and box up books early on in the game; then later, Patty, who helped pack up clothing and other stuff as moving day drew near—I still massively failed in being able to manage it all. And by "all," I mean all the excessive accumulation of material possessions I'd amassed.

The worst of it had to do with a "Clean Sweep" attempt that went south. And by "south," I don't mean on a vacation to a tropical climate!

I'd read a library book about how they do a "Clean Sweep" on the reality TV show of that name. I'd never seen the show but was intrigued by the idea and thought I could do my own "Clean Sweep." Planning ahead, I bought new tarps so I could put everything on tarps (just like they did in the book) as the items came from out of the house.

My target room was my "office," which had become nothing but a clogged junk room. Why is it that the American "home office" is so often the room that morphs into a junk room? I suppose if rooms were drawers, the home office must be the "junk drawer."

To save steps in transporting everything out of that room, I rigged up a ramp going from a window down to the backyard. My daughter, bless her heart, helped me with Phase 1 of my "Clean Sweep" by passing items out the window, one at a time, onto the window ramp. I stood outside the window, receiving each item, carrying everything out to the tarps on the lawn. It was a long, arduous, and challenging process. I cried. (It's not easy confronting the truth when things get so out-of-hand.) By the time we got everything out of the office, laid out on tarps in the backyard, I was emotionally drained and physically exhausted.

The weather in our intense four-season climate suddenly turned to scorching hot. Everything stayed out there, sandwiched between tarps, cooking in the hot sun, while I waited for cooler weather in which to sort through it all. But as soon as it wasn't too hot, it was *raining*. When the rainy season ended, it was *freezing* and snowing. So much for naïvely thinking I could do a "Clean Sweep" all by myself!

It wasn't until I met Ceci Garrett (hoarding coach and founder of Lighten the Load ministry in Spokane, Washington) that I learned reality TV shows like Clean

Sweep involve a whole TEAM of strong people who move all the clutter and load it in trucks to haul away. A real Clean Sweep, as done in the TV show, is not a one-woman job.

Even though it had all been "protected" by tarps, after a year of that stuff remaining stuck out in the weather, of course, it was all ruined. There really aren't words to describe the anguish and humiliation I felt. What had been a major problem I'd been avoiding dealing with *inside* had become a HUGE problem *outside*. I finally had no choice but to deal with it. I couldn't just "fuh gedda bow dit."

So ashamed was I of the gross failure of my botched "Clean Sweep," I wouldn't even allow my husband to help me with the decomposing mess of it all. I didn't want anyone else to witness, or be subjected to, the disastrous, pathetic mess. I had created that mess, and I was going to face up to it.

The discarding process that ensued was the session I was referring to in Chapter 5: "Get More Done by Working Together," when I needed to enlist the help of an accountability coach. In addition to a scheduled start time that included a check-in with my coach at the agreed-upon time, I also had at my disposal an empty trailer in which to put all the ruined stuff, so my husband could haul it to the dump.

From start to finish, my grossly failed attempt at a "Clean Sweep" was a deeply humiliating experience. My only consolation—as I worked through the demoralizing process of shoveling with a pitchfork all my ruined "treasures" into a trailer destined for the dump—was the truth in what the apostle Paul told Timothy: "**After all, we brought nothing with us when we came into the world, and we can't take anything with us when we leave it**" (1 Timothy 6:7, NLT).

That humbling experience was, to me, a death of sorts. I was grieving all the way through it.

It's been a number of years since *My Big Clean Sweep* fiasco. Whenever I glimpse back at it with a shudder of remembrance, I am once again reminded of Paul's words to Timothy:

> **"What did we bring into this world? Nothing! What can we take out of the world? Nothing!"**
> —1 Timothy 6:7, GNT

PRAYER

Thank You, Lord, that when we leave this world, we won't need to take anything with us. You are all I need, now and forever. Help me to recognize what is excess in my life now, so that I can travel lighter on this earth until You call me Home. Help me, Lord, to have an eternal perspective regarding my possessions. In Jesus' Name. Amen.

TAKE ACTION

- Do you have a potted plant that has become rootbound? If so, find a suitable, larger pot with a drainage hole. Then, transplant the rootbound plant, using fresh potting soil. Sweep up any spilled potting soil, and discard the old container.

- Do you have a room in your house that has become "rootbound"—cramped and tangled with too much stuff that has outgrown the space? Write it down here:

FOLLOW THESE ACTION STEPS TO TACKLE THAT "ROOTBOUND" ROOM

1. Begin with confession. Before doing anything else, repent for the part you played in letting that tangled up space get to the state it's in. Confess your sin to God. Write it down here:

2. Tell God what you want to accomplish in that space and why. Write down your "what" and "why" here:

3. Pray to God for guidance: "Show me what to do, because my prayers go up to you."[1]

4. Will you need help dealing with this "rootbound" space? If so, ask the Holy Spirit to bring to mind the name of someone who might be willing and able to help you detangle that room. Write the name of who you plan to ask for help here:

5. Call that person and ask for help. Together, set a date and time for a decluttering session together. Write your scheduled appointment here; and also mark it on your calendar/planner/phone.

   If you'll be working alone, write your appointment with yourself here; and mark it on your calendar/planner/phone. Then ask for accountability with someone by making a phone appointment for that person to call you at the start time of your scheduled decluttering appointment with yourself, to make sure you're following through on what you purposed to do.

6. <u>Make a plan of attack:</u>

Decide how your helper (if working with one) can best assist you. (Refer to Chapter 5: Get More Done by Working Together.)

Whether you'll be working alone, or with a helper, decide what section of the room you'll start with and how you will proceed from there.

GATHER YOUR SUPPLIES

- Four boxes labeled: "Give Away," "Throw Away," "Put Away," and "Repair or Return."
- Garbage bag for lining the "Throw Away" box.
- Your list of Sorting and Discarding Questions. (See Chapter 11: In the Valley of Decision.)
- A dust rag

7. On the day of your scheduled decluttering session, pray the prayer in Chapter 15: When Clutter Becomes a Spiritual Battle.

8. Go through the entire room, putting items that don't belong in that room into the four boxes. Refer to your list of Sorting and Discarding Questions as needed. When the room has been completely sorted and purged of unnecessary stuff, deal with those four boxes:

- Dump the trash in the "Throw Away" box into the garbage bin outside.
- Put the "Give Away" box in the trunk of your car to deposit at a local donation center. Make a reminder note on your calendar/planner/phone to drop it off the next time you are running errands.
- Put the items in the "Put Away" box back in the other rooms where they belong.
- Put the items in the "Repair or Return" box in your car, so you can take them to be fixed, or return them to the library, or store, or person they belong to.
- Make a reminder note on your calendar/planner/phone to deal with these the next time you are running errands.

9. When you have completed the decluttering of that "rootbound" room, write the name of that room here, and the word, *"Done!"* Sign your name and write the date it was completed.

10. Do something fun to celebrate your success.

To learn about "non-acquiring" ways to celebrate, and for an invitation to take a special kind of break, read Chapter 20: **More Than Enough**.

PART THREE
Saying No to More

"When you have Enough, you have everything you need. There's nothing extra to weigh you down, distract, or distress you...
...To let go of clutter, then, is not deprivation; it's lightening up and opening up space and time for something new and wonderful to happen." ~ Vicki Robin, *Your Money or Your Life*

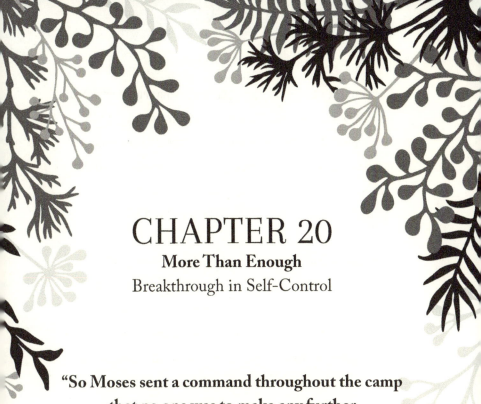

CHAPTER 20
More Than Enough
Breakthrough in Self-Control

"So Moses sent a command throughout the camp
that no one was to make any further
contribution for the sacred Tent;
so the people did not bring any more.
What had already been brought was more
than enough to finish all the work."
—Exodus 36:6-8, GNT

"…for the stuff they had was sufficient
to do all the work, and more."
—Exodus 36:7, RSV

As God began the process of delivering me from material addiction (addiction to material things and "stuff") about 15 years ago, I wrote the following:

For a week now, God has been preparing my heart for a fast: A season in which I am to abstain from the act of accumulating. (Which will mean: no recreational shopping, no yard-saling, no garage-saling, no thrift-shopping, no Jo-Ann's Fabrics, and no library usage.) God wants to prove to me that I already have MORE THAN ENOUGH.

I already have more than enough books, clothes, paints, fabrics, magazines, plants, wallpaper, dishes, education, information, ideas, knowledge. Like He did with Abraham, God wants to prove to me that I can go "up on the mountain," so to speak, and know that God will provide.¹ And, in fact, He already has, abundantly. God has already provided me with so much, not only in the way of material possessions, but in gifts and talents, as well as the priceless blessings of my husband and children. I already have MORE THAN ENOUGH. I don't need to accumulate another thing in order to experience God's blessings in my life.

So, thankfully, God is setting these boundaries for me, so that I can break free of material addiction. In addition to feeling somewhat apprehensive, I am also feeling relieved that God is giving me this opportunity to take a break from endless accumulating. Without the constant distraction of always acquiring more stuff, I will be able to enjoy utilizing the generous stores of all that God has already provided. I don't need to bring anything more into this house.

Moses had to set similar boundaries for the Israelites, because, when they were bringing supplies and things for the building and beautification of the Holy Tent, they didn't know when to stop.[2] They were like happy little songbirds feathering their nest.

For us Messy-a.n.i.c. Christian women, it can be tempting to go a little overboard in our own "nesting." If we're not careful, it's easy to fall into a pattern of over-accumulation, amassing more supplies and home beautification objects than we really need. If you find yourself in a similar situation, perhaps it's time to observe a period of abstinence—abstinence from acquiring anything more.

The Israelites were happy to be contributing to the sanctuary project—the creation of the Meeting Tent—and all the things in it, including the special clothes. They gladly brought all kinds of jewelry, precious metals, colored threads, textiles, dyed sheepskins, jewels, stones, and special oils.[3]

As homemakers desiring to set up and beautify our own "tent," to create our own sanctuary, we, too, bring gifts to our home—in the way of curtains, throw rugs, scented candles, linens, clothing, jewelry, and more. But who will be our "Moses" when all the stuff has become "more than enough"?

If you can see yourself in this biblical account from Exodus and know that the stuff you have at this point is sufficient and "more than enough," I give you permission to STOP. Stop bringing more stuff into your "tent." I invite you to take a break from accumulating, from acquiring more stuff. Take a lovely, relaxing holiday from bringing more possessions into your "tent," your sanctuary.

> **"At this time you have plenty.
> What you have can help others who are in need."**
> —2 Corinthians 8:14a

PRAYER

Dear Jesus, thank You for so generously providing for all my needs and the needs of my family. Help me to continue to trust in Your provision, Lord. Give me the strength and self-control to resist the temptation to accumulate more unnecessary clutter in my life. Help me to be 100% satisfied with the abundant riches and blessings You've already given me. In Your Holy Name, I pray. Amen.

TAKE ACTION

1) List God's provision …

Five areas in my life in which God has *already* provided:
1.
2.
3.
4.
5.

**"I will sing to the Lord,
because He has dealt bountifully with me."**
—Psalm 13:6

2) If the Lord has dealt bountifully with you and you have more than enough, out of your bounty, gather items you don't need and make a donation to your local thrift store or to someone in need.

**"Please take this gift I have brought you,
for God has been very gracious to me.
I have more than enough."**
—Genesis 33:11a, NLT

3) If the Lord is leading you to do so, commit to honoring Him with a 40-day fast—a season of abstinence from shopping, acquiring, or accumulating any more stuff. Mark it on your calendar. Draw a star or a happy face, or put a small sticker, on each day of your calendar in which you abstain from the act of accumulating.

> For a free downloadable **Chart for the 40-Day Fast**, go to: http://bit.ly/MessyanicActionGuide.

4) Plan out what you will do to celebrate the completion of your 40-day fast. (Non-acquiring ways to celebrate might be to go out for dinner, rent a funny movie, have a pedicure, or go for a massage. In other words, anything but shopping.)

Write down here how you plan to celebrate the successful completion of your 40-Day Fast:

5) Then, when you've completed the 40-day fast—40-days in which you will have abstained from the act of accumulating—praise the Lord and do something *non-acquiring* to celebrate!

Read Chapter 21 to learn how *self-sufficiency can become a stumbling block* to meeting your goals for a tidy, clutter-free home.

CHAPTER 21
Physical Preparedness vs. Spiritual Readiness
Breakthrough in Trust

"… I go to prepare a place for you …"
—from John 14:3, CEB

Jesus is the original Prepper. He told His disciples, **"Don't be troubled. Trust in God. Trust also in Me. My Father's house has room to spare. If that weren't the case, would I have told you that I'm going to prepare a place for you? When I go to prepare a place for you, I will return and take you to be with Me so that where I am you will be too"** (John 14:1-3, CEB). So, it's only natural, having been made in the image of God,[1] that we would have a built-in natural tendency to be planners and preparers.

Even with all of my ADD-related struggles with maintenance routines and clutter, I am a natural-born planner/organizer from way back. When I was growing up, I planned my own birthday parties, staged talent shows, choreographed dance performances, and even planned and organized my own summer day camp for the younger children in my neighborhood. As a young, married woman and mother, I planned menus, parties, holidays, and vacations. As a dance studio teacher, I planned and prepared dance routines, costumes, and recitals. As a dance/movement artist-in-the-schools, I planned and prepared lesson plans and classroom curriculum for teaching basic subjects through creative movement in elementary school classrooms.

Somewhere along the way, though I'm not quite sure how it happened, my God-given penchant for planning and organizing got side-tracked by the enemy. Instead of planning and preparing for ways to bless others, I got sucked into a fear-based mindset, believing that I needed to be like Joseph planning and preparing for the seven-year famine in Egypt.[2] Convinced that I was being a good little "ant," storing up food and gathering supplies,[3] my zeal fueled by authors and speakers on the topic of "preparedness," I became increasingly concerned with trying to plan and prepare for every possible anticipated need that might arise in the event of an economic collapse.

My efforts never fully achieved complete perfection, however, because once you go down that rabbit hole, there is no end in sight. A preoccupation with preparedness can never be fully satisfied. There is always something else that needs to be acquired and stored for that supposedly inevitable day W.T.S.H.T.F.

Although romantic at first, in a *Little House on the Prairie* sort of way, the mentality of having to be fully self-reliant and self-sufficient can become an idol. Instead of trusting and relying on God for my provision, I was basically trying to be my own god, putting all my trust and reliance on my own efforts to plan and prepare for whatever the future might bring.

It wasn't until I sought the Lord for help with my clutter problem that the Holy Spirit showed me how my drive to be "self-sufficient" was actually contributing to my clutter problem. Although I sometimes still struggle with finding the right balance in determining what is a reasonable amount of supplies to have on hand for day-to-day use, I no longer feel compelled to stockpile enough provisions to last into eternity. I don't have to, because preparations are already being made for a place for us. I can now rest in the comfort of knowing that a place is being prepared, in which we will enjoy eternity.

"... I go to prepare a place for you ..."
—from John 14:3, CEB

PRAYER

Forgive me, Lord, for the times I have become sidetracked by the concerns of this world. Forgive me for the times I have forgotten that it is *You* who prepares a place for me. I repent, Lord, for my lack of faith that contributed to an over-accumulation of supplies for this life on earth. I realize that striving to be self-reliant or self-sufficient prevented me from being fully reliant on You.

You alone are my Sufficiency. Help me, Lord, to not obsess about physical preparedness, but to be more concerned with spiritual readiness. I want to be ready, Lord, for spending eternity in Heaven with You, in the place you are preparing for me. In Jesus' Name. Amen.

Jesus Has Your Back
Exercise in Trust

Remember that old trust exercise (dare) in which you're supposed to fall backward, trusting that your friend or partner will catch you? In that game, there's no guarantee that the other person will be able to break your fall and catch you. We're just supposed to *trust*, hoping they're big enough and strong enough; whereas, with *God*, we never have to worry. He is always big enough and strong enough. God is entirely able and trustworthy. He always has your back.

As an exercise in faith, to strengthen your trust in God's provision, I challenge you to start running out of stuff. If you're a "stock-up" Messy-a.n.i.c. Christian woman, chances are, you seldom run out of essentials. You probably have backup supplies. Especially given today's B.O.G.O. marketing strategies.

Side note: I once told the women in my Bible study group that I draw the line at toilet paper. I've always said there are two things I try to never run out of: toilet paper and butter! ("I have my priorities!") One of the women, a kind neighbor of mine, offered, "You could always just come around the corner and borrow a roll from me!" That was a lightbulb moment. A perfectly simple example of how God takes care of His own—right down to the toilet paper.

On that note, for the remainder of our 40-Day Fast, I challenge you to refrain from buying any necessities until you run out. The exercise here is to practice running out of things. It won't be the end of the world if you run out of toothpaste, shampoo, or coffee creamer. This exercise is to help us reset/reframe our mindset of thinking we always have to have backup provisions on hand ... to put to rest that old, fear-based mentality of always anticipating everything we might ever need, in case, God forbid, we should run out! This exercise is also to remind ourselves that we don't have to be God, that we are not the Provider. God is.

Think of Abraham's faith when he trusted God to provide, as he prepared to sacrifice his own son, Isaac. At the last moment, God stopped him and provided a ram for the sacrifice. That's when Abraham named that place Jehovah-Jireh, which means The Lord Will Provide. Or, in other words, *Jesus Has Your Back.*

TAKE ACTION

- If "prepping" has ever been a stumbling block for you, get out whatever "preparedness" or "survival" materials (such as books and/or DVDs) you have, and ask the Holy Spirit which, if any, of them you need to keep. Discard any that have become a deterrent to you from fully relying on God as your Provider. Do the same with any e-books or other downloaded resources you might have on the subject of preparedness/survival/self-reliance. Or...

- If this issue has not ever been a problem for you, go to your "guest room," if you have one, as if you were going to prepare a place for Jesus to be an overnight visitor in your home. Consider what changes, if any, need to be made to that space for it to be a welcoming place for Him to rest. Is the area clean? Is there any junk that needs to be removed? Is the guest bed clear of any stray clutter? Is there a bedside lamp and a Bible at hand?

(Messy-a.n.i.c. Praise Report: I have a little storage cabinet on the wall above my toilet, which can hold 32 rolls of toilet paper. When supplies are dwindling, and my favorite brand of T.P. is on sale, I will usually buy a package or two to replenish the cupboard. But since writing this chapter, I decided to "go for broke" and waited until the cabinet was completely empty before buying more. For a recovering stocker-upper, that exercise gave me opportunity to practice trusting God for provision, instead of trying to be my own goddess of provision. The next exercise in trust I'll be putting into practice: running out of butter!)

Read Chapter 22: **Jesus Is My Superpower**
to learn about power in *Dependence!*

CHAPTER 22
Jesus Is My Superpower
Breakthrough in Dependence

> "With Your help I can attack an army.
> With God's help I can jump over a wall."
> —Psalm 18:29

In the original Superman movies, there was always an introduction by an announcer, proclaiming how the superhero was "faster than a speeding bullet, more powerful than a locomotive, and able to leap tall buildings at a single bound" because he had supernatural powers "far beyond those of mortal men."

The idea of a superhero with superpowers is something we are instinctively drawn to. This is likely because, deep down, as mere mortals, we yearn for someone who can come in and "save the day"! We are hard-wired by design to crave a higher power, a Savior.

Unfortunately, I spent 25 years of my life trying to be my own higher power—trying to fix myself, heal myself, save myself. In fact, before I was saved, I had been working on my doctoral dissertation on "Integrative Self-Healing." But when I accepted Christ as my Lord and Savior, the veil of deception fell away, and I knew the truth: There is no healing without Jesus Christ.

No matter how hard we try, we can't fix ourselves, heal ourselves, or save ourselves from the mess we've made of things. Yet, we live in a D.I.Y. world of self-help books, blogs, seminars, and retreats. The crazy thing is, until we embrace the fact that all healing comes through Christ, we can never get enough of whatever new system or ideology promises to empower us to "create our own reality." The pursuit of "enlightenment," "inner peace," or "self-actualization" can become an all-consuming obsession.

"These women are always learning new teachings, but they are never able to understand the truth fully."
—2 Timothy 3:7

No matter how fervently we seek fulfillment, or how devotedly we try to achieve our ideal life, ultimately, there will be no satisfaction as long as we insist on doing it without God. And not just any god. Only the One True God, the Creator of the Universe, has the power to change us from the inside out. On our own, we are powerless.

The apostle Paul told the church in Rome,

> **"I do not understand my own actions.
> For I do not do what I want,
> but I do the very thing I hate....
> I want to do the things that are good,
> but I do not do them.
> I do not do the good things I want to do,
> but I do the bad things I do not want to do."**
> —Romans 7:15, 18b-19

When you read these words of confession by Paul, what comes to mind for you, in terms of your struggle with clutter? For me, some of the things I *want* to do (but too often don't do) are:

- Consistently follow daily and weekly maintenance routines.
- Establish organizational systems for dealing with paperwork.
- Have a place for everything, and everything in its place.
- Keep nothing that I do not find to be beautiful or useful.
- Only keep those things that "spark joy" in me.
- Plan weekly menus and meal plans.

- Create a budget and stick to it.

Some of the things I do *not* want to do, but too often find myself doing, are:
- Procrastinating.
- Setting things down where they don't belong, "for now," because I don't have a designated place for them.
- Letting things pile up.
- Avoiding dealing with difficult or unpleasant tasks.
- Holding onto unread magazines or unfinished projects, thinking I'll get around to them, but never do.
- Scrambling to pay a bill on the last day it's due because I don't have a good system for dealing with paperwork.
- Sending out birthday or Christmas cards late (or not at all) because I didn't take the time to sit down and deal with them earlier.

Yup, just like the apostle Paul, **"I want to do the things that are good, but I do not do them. I do not do the good things I want to do, but I do the bad things I do not want to do"** (Romans 7:18b-19).

What are the things you *want* to do, but have trouble making yourself do? List them here:

What are the unhelpful or unproductive things you do *not* want to do, but do them anyway? List them here:

Just like the apostle Paul, we struggle with a sin nature. That's why we need our Higher Power, Jesus Christ. With His help, we can attack an army of spiritual enemies. With God's help, we can jump over a wall of clutter.

> **"Don't be afraid or distressed by this great horde; for the battle is not yours, but God's."**
> —2 Chronicles 20:15b, CJB

> **"The Lord says, 'Don't be afraid! Don't be paralyzed by this mighty army! For the battle is not yours, but God's!'"**
> —2 Chronicles 20:15b, TLB

PRAYER

Lord, thank You for Your Word that shows me I am not alone in my struggle to do the things I want to do and not do the things I don't want to do. Without You, I am powerless. I am powerless to fix myself or change myself. I am completely dependent on You, Lord, and Your life-giving, life-saving, life-changing power.

Lord, I've tried for so long to fix and change myself, with no real, lasting success. If I could have done it on my own, I would have done it by now. So, I completely surrender all of my clutter and all of my personal quirks and habits that have contributed to the situation I'm in now. I feel scared, Lord, but I trust that You love me unconditionally, in spite of my shortcomings or my messy home. I ask You to change me from the inside out. Lord, since I have many spiritual enemies, show me clearly how You want me to live (Psalm 5:8).

Help me, Lord, to do the things I need to do to make an improved and lasting difference in my home environment so that I can be a better ambassador for You by fulfilling my ministry of hospitality. In Your Holy Name, I pray. Amen.

TAKE ACTION

Choose one thing from your list of things you want to do, but have trouble making yourself do. Write it down here; *then do it.*

When that thing is done, thank God for His power that helped you do it. Then come back to this page and write: *Done!* Sign your name and write the date it was done.

<u>God's Promise:</u>
"I am the Lord your God, who holds your right hand, and I tell you, 'Don't be afraid. I will help you.'"
—Isaiah 41:13

Read Chapter 23: **A Pile to Remind Us**
for a *Breakthrough in Accessibility.*

CHAPTER 23
A Pile to Remind Us
Breakthrough in Accessibility

> "…then they ate beside the pile.
> Laban named that place in his language
> A Pile to Remind Us,
> and Jacob gave the same name in Hebrew.
> Laban said to Jacob,
> 'This pile of rocks will remind us of
> the agreement between us.'
> That is why the place was called
> A Pile to Remind Us."
> —Genesis 31:46b-48

I once knew a fellow gardener/plant lover in my old garden club, "The Sisterhood of the Traveling Plants," who described her overly abundant (and as yet unplanted) assortment of botanical acquisitions as her "Pile of Shame." Granted, the rock pile assembled by Jacob and his relatives was not a reminder of shame, but more of a boundary marker. It served as a visual reminder of their separation from one another.[1]

Jacob's father-in-law dubbed it "A Pile to Remind Us" so they would both be reminded to not go past the rock pile to harm one another. And they both had good cause to need such a reminder. After Laban had cheated and taken advantage of Jacob repeatedly for 20 years, Jacob finally decided he'd had enough; so, he and his wives and children ditched the old man. Consequently, Laban was ticked off. To top it all off, when he found out that his son-in-law, daughters, and grandchildren had run away, he discovered that his idols had been stolen. With so much mistrust and animosity between Jacob and Laban, "A Pile to Remind Us" was probably a good idea in that situation.[2]

In my own situation, I didn't intentionally set out to erect "A Pile to Remind Us." Nevertheless, I've found myself surrounded by stacks and piles (of clothes, books, and paper clutter) that serve as ever-present visual reminders of my struggle with clutter.

Piles like this *do* "Remind Us." They remind us of our need for boundaries concerning the question, "How much is enough?" They also remind us of all the work we need to do to tackle those piles of clutter, chaos, and deferred decisions. Like the rock pile these Old Testament men built was a monument to remind them to stay away from one another, our piles of clutter also separate us from one another. In other words, having "A Pile (of Stuff) to Remind Us" becomes a sort of boundary or barrier, because we are less likely to fulfill our ministry of hospitality when we are self-conscious of the state of our personal space.

In reading about Jacob and Laban's "Pile to Remind Us," are you reminded of a particularly troubling pile in your own environment that causes you to keep people away, for fear of what they might think? Or is there a pile of clutter somewhere in your home that prevents you from being able to access a particular area, such as a certain drawer, table, closet, or room? Let's take it to the Lord in …

PRAYER

Forgive me, Lord. I didn't set out to create "A Pile to Remind Us." It was never my intention to allow things to get to the point of keeping people at a distance. I know I need to have more clearly defined boundaries for myself about how much is enough. But being surrounded by stacks and piles of stuff is not the kind of boundary I need. Because when I have too much clutter, it becomes a barrier in my life, causing me to keep even good, safe people away, for fear of what they might think of me and my struggle with clutter.

Help me, Lord, to dismantle the piles of clutter in my life. The prospect of tackling such a large undertaking feels daunting—as heavy as trying to move the large stones in Jacob's and Laban's rock pile. But I know that is just a trick of the enemy trying to keep me from knocking it down.

Thank You, Lord, that just as You promised Israel in Isaiah 40:4, "**... every mountain and hill should be made flat ... [and] ... the rough ground should be made level, and the rugged ground should be made smooth,**" by Your Power, God, every clutter pile "should be made flat" and the cluttered floor "should be made smooth."

From now on, by Your Grace, may my only "Pile of Shame" be the pile of my sins at the foot of the cross. In Jesus' Name. Amen.

> **"Every valley will be raised.**
> **Every mountain and hill will be lowered.**
> **Steep places will be made level.**
> **Rough places will be made smooth."**
> —Isaiah 40:4, GWT

TAKE ACTION

1) In Genesis 31:46b, it says that Jacob and Laban "ate beside the pile." Is there a pile of paper clutter on your dining table? Or a pile of miscellaneous clutter in your dining room? Rather than eating "beside the pile," ask God to give you the strength and clarity of mind to dismantle it. Guesstimate how long you think it will take. Gather whatever supplies you think you'll need (such as trash bag, paper shredder, file folders, scanner, etc.). Set a timer for however long you think it will take, and dive in. If you have a hard time making yourself do mundane tasks, and you need more support, either get a trusted friend to sit with you during your sorting and clearing session or text a trusted friend and ask her to be praying for you as you clear out "the pile."

2) Once "the pile" is gone, invite someone over for a cup of coffee and a bite to eat.

3) Repeat this Action Step for any other areas in your home where you eat "beside the pile."

4) Praise God that you no longer have to eat "beside the pile!"

For a Breakthrough in Contentment,
read Chapter 24:
I Have Everything I Need.

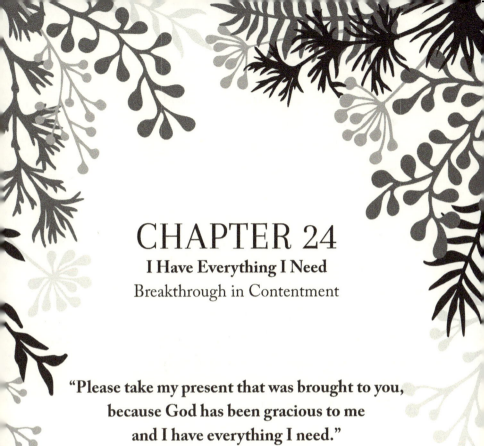

CHAPTER 24
I Have Everything I Need
Breakthrough in Contentment

"Please take my present that was brought to you, because God has been gracious to me and I have everything I need."
—Genesis 33:11a, CSB

The above scripture from Genesis is from an encounter between two estranged brothers, Jacob and Esau, in which each declared to the other, "I already have enough," and, "I have more than I need."[1]

Recently there has been a popular list circulating on Facebook titled, "10 Signs You're Doing Well in Life."[2, 3, 4, 5] Half of the ten items on the list are intangible, priceless things money can't buy. The other five are basic needs:

- "You have a roof over your head."
- "You ate today."
- "You have clean water."
- "You have clean clothes."
- "You're breathing."

Like Jacob and Esau, I, too, have enough. God has indeed been gracious to me. I have a roof over my head, clothing with which to cover myself, a pot of soup on the stove, oil in the furnace, wood for the fireplace, a bed to sleep on, water for washing, people who love me, a wonderful church home-and-family in the body of Christ, and God's promise of everlasting life with Him in an eternal home in Heaven.

All of the other stuff—cosmetics, jewelry, TV, books, magazines, radio, movies, and the myriad miscellaneous items we love to shop for and accumulate—is just *stuff*. Stuff to distract us from what's really important in life. Stuff to take our eyes off of eternity, and to get us caught up in temporal cares, concerns, and pleasures instead.

How freeing it would be for us to have less *stuff* and more *Jesus* in our life!

PRAYER

Lord, the next time I am tempted to acquire more stuff, help me to remember that—like Esau and Jacob—I, too, have enough. Thank You, Lord, for having dealt so graciously with me. Thank You for all the many blessings You have already given me. Lord, help me to be content with less stuff so that there will be room for more of *You* in my life. In Jesus' Name, I pray. Amen.

TAKE ACTION

1) Identify one or two kinds of "stuff" that you may have accumulated too much of. Write it down here:

    I have too much _____

    _____.

2) Schedule an appointment with yourself in which to go through those one or two kinds of "stuff" and discard the excess. Write your sorting and discarding appointment commitment down here:

    Date:_____Time: _____

3) When you have completed the task, make a note of your accomplishment here, and praise the Lord!

**And now I have everything, and more.
I have all I need…**
— from Philippians 4:18

(Messy-a.n.i.c. Praise Report: Both my husband and I are avid readers; consequently, we have an abundance of books. To create an outlet for giving away our surplus books, my husband built and installed a "Little Free Library" near the sidewalk alongside our garden. Now we enjoy sharing free books with all of our neighbors and the travelers who hike through this area.)

Read Chapter 25: **The Wilderness of Sin** to learn about stages of progress in your journey from clutter bondage to recovery.

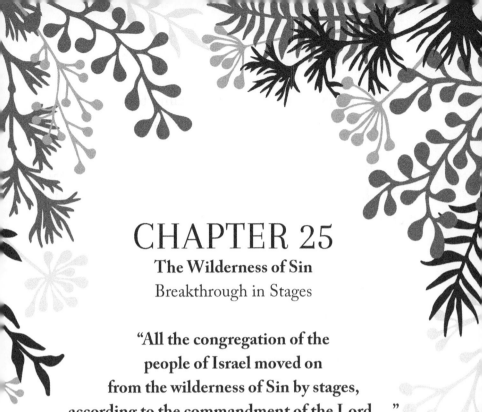

CHAPTER 25
The Wilderness of Sin
Breakthrough in Stages

*"All the congregation of the
people of Israel moved on
from the wilderness of Sin by stages,
according to the commandment of the Lord …"*
—Exodus 17:1a ESV

Although God delivered the Israelites out of bondage with one mighty parting of the Red Sea, they then had to press on through the wilderness of Sin.[1,2,3] When it came time for them to pull up their tent pegs and move on, God gave specific instructions for how they were to move on—in a systematic, orderly way, one stage at a time.

What is *your* "wilderness of Sin?" Whether we are moving on from an unhealthy relationship, dealing with grief over the death/loss of a loved one, or overcoming an addiction, we can expect the healing to be a gradual process. Recovery occurs in stages. It's a process.

In dealing with recovery from a clutter disorder, God first delivers us out of the spiritual bondage of the addiction. *Then* begins the journey of moving on by stages.

This might mean choosing to say "No" when a friend invites you along for some "recreational" shopping or "retail therapy" at your favorite second-hand stores. It might mean attending some type of "Clutter Control Clinic" in the city where you live, or getting a trusted friend to help you purge your junk room or edit your closet or bookcases. It might mean having a yard sale to thin out your inventory of possessions or calling a local charity to come and pick up your giveaway "treasures."

As we move on **"from the wilderness of Sin by stages, according to the commandment of the Lord,"**[4] each action step we take brings us that much closer to *our* "land of milk and honey," that is, restored order and a more serene and clutter-free life.

PRAYER

Dear Jesus, Thank You for delivering me from the spiritual bondage of clutter addiction. And thank You for each stage of the journey as You guide me out of the "wilderness of Sin." I praise You for all the good You are doing in me and in my home.

Help me, Lord, to recognize and celebrate each step of the way, as I move in stages toward a more serene and clutter-free life. In Your Holy Name, I pray. Amen.

TAKE ACTION

1) What are some of the "stages" of progress that you would like to see completed in your continued journey towards a more serene and clutter-free home? (Some examples might be as follows: spices sorted/decluttered and organized; jewelry sorted/decluttered and organized; Xmas storage totes sorted/decluttered and organized.)

   List those different "stages" of progress here:

2) What are some "non-acquiring"* ways you can continue to celebrate small steps of progress towards a more serene and clutter-free life? (Some examples might be, "Giving myself a manicure," "Finishing a craft project," "Watching a funny movie," or "Going out for an ice cream cone."

*"*Non-acquiring" means activities that do not involve shopping or acquiring more stuff.*

Write your list of (non-acquiring) **Ways to Celebrate** your small progress steps here:

3) Choose one task from your list of "stages" above and one non-acquiring way to celebrate from your list above. Make a date with yourself for both the task and the celebration. Write them on

your calendar, add them to your phone calendar, and set reminders on your phone. Then, have fun as you continue in your journey to restored order and serenity, in your heart and in your home.

**Continue to do those things;
give your life to doing them so that
your progress may be seen by everyone.**
—1 Timothy 4:15

Read Chapter 26 to see how
God has been changing you from the inside out,
in: **Looking Forward to the Future with Joy!**

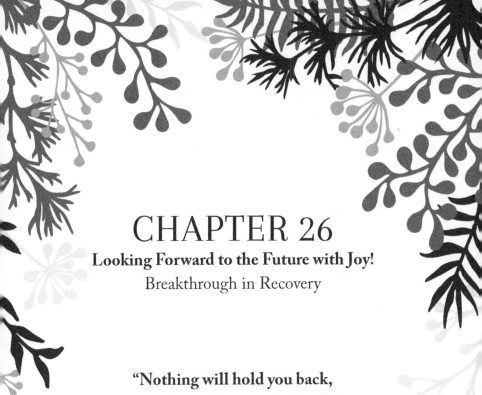

CHAPTER 26
Looking Forward to the Future with Joy!
Breakthrough in Recovery

"Nothing will hold you back,
you will not be overwhelmed."
—Proverbs 4:12

"She looks forward to the future with joy."
—Proverbs 31:25b

If you have worked through this book up to this point—reading, praying the prayers, and taking action with the application steps—you are not the same person you were before you started this journey. God has been changing you from the inside out. As a result, together, by the Power and Grace of God…

… We've broken through the debilitating shame
and embarrassment associated with clutter.
**"Don't be afraid, because you will not be ashamed.
Don't be embarrassed, because
you will not be disgraced.
You will forget the shame you felt earlier …"**
—Isaiah 54:4

… We've dealt with the debris of our past.
"You give me a better way to live."
—Psalm 18:36a

… We've sought help from God and others.
**"Two people are better than one,
because they get more done by working together."**
—Ecclesiastes 4:9
"The Lord is beside you to help you."
—Psalm 110:5a

… We've been delivered from our enemies:
Chaos, Confusion, Indecision, Overwhelmment,
Lethargy, Inertia, Emotional/Mental
Paralysis, Shame, Fear, Guilt, Avoidance.
**"The Lord has stopped punishing you.
He has sent your enemies away."**
—Zephaniah 3:15a

... We've rejected the lies of the enemy.
**"And you will know the truth,
and the truth will set you free."**
—John 8:32

... We've been able to forgive ourselves.
**"... and you will not be accused of being guilty.
Forgive, and you will be forgiven."**
—Luke 6:37b
**"There is therefore now no condemnation
for those who are in Christ Jesus."**
—Romans 8:1, RSV

... We've taken a stand and moved out of the paralyzing inertia of overwhelmment.
**"Nothing will hold you back,
you will not be overwhelmed."**
—Proverbs 4:12

... We've repented and learned how to be content with what we have.
"... for I have learned how to be content with whatever I have."
—Philippians 4:11b, NLT

... We've sought the Lord's guidance and have made a lot of liberating decisions.
"People throw lots to make a decision,

but the answer comes from the Lord."
—Proverbs 16:33

… We've learned to let go of things;
and we've released and relinquished
a lot of unnecessary stuff.
"Your heart will be where your treasure is."
—Luke 12:34; Matthew 6:21

… We've gained a new, eternal
perspective on possessions.
**"We didn't bring anything into this world,
and we won't take anything with us when we leave."**
—1 Timothy 6:7, CEV

… We've been able to bless others with our excess.
**"At this time you have plenty.
What you have can help others who are in need."**
—2 Corinthians 8:14a

… We've counted our blessings.
**"I will sing to the Lord,
because He has dealt bountifully with me."**
—Psalm 13:6

… We've fasted from acquiring and accumulating.
**"Then Jesus said to them,
'Be careful and guard against all kinds of greed.**

Life is not measured by how much one owns.'"
—Luke 12:15

… We've started creating new, simple, daily maintenance habits; and we've made a plan for continued progress in decluttering and restoring order and serenity to our homes.
"But let everything be done in a right and orderly way."
—1 Corinthians 14:40

… We've made plans for non-acquiring ways of celebrating the continuing stages of victory in the sanctification process in our hearts and homes.
"And all people should eat and drink and enjoy the fruits of their labor, for these are gifts from God."
—Ecclesiastes 3:13, NLT

Finally, we are enjoying newfound contentment in the midst of the mess that is known as ***LIFE!***

It is my prayer that as you continue in your Messy-a.n.i.c. Christian walk through life, you will return to this study as often as needed to be richly rewarded by the Lord's blessings as you pray these prayers and continue to take action in the application steps.

Thank you for taking this journey with me in your spiritual recovery from clutter bondage, so that, together, we can boldly invite Jesus into our Messy-a.n.i.c. hearts and homes, saying,

"Come in, Lord, please excuse the mess!"

TAKE ACTION

- If you have found this book to be beneficial in your Messy-a.n.i.c. walk with the Lord and would like to share it with others, I encourage you to share this study with the women at your church. Invite the women in your church to join together in this *Messy-a.n.i.c. Christian Study for Recovery from Clutter Bondage* by having a **Come In, Lord, Please Excuse the Mess!** weekly group study at your church.

To download
Group Study Format with Leader Guidelines,
go to: http://bit.ly/MessyanicActionGuide.

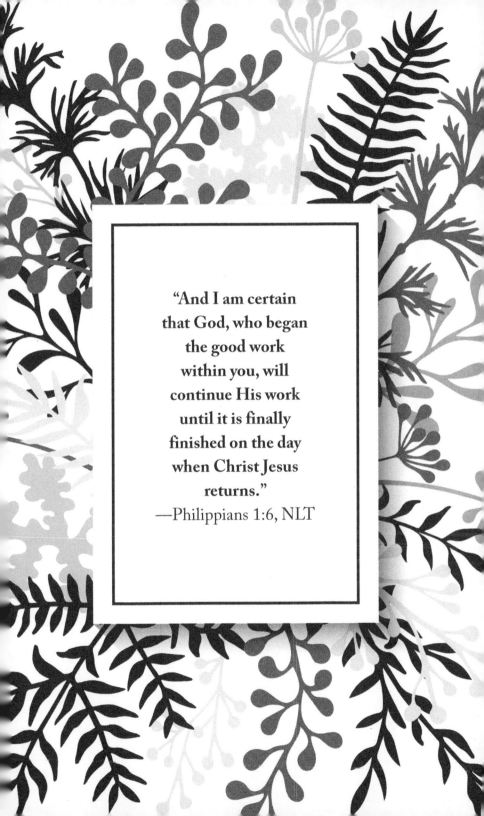

"And I am certain that God, who began the good work within you, will continue His work until it is finally finished on the day when Christ Jesus returns."
—Philippians 1:6, NLT

ENDNOTES:

Chapter 1: Come In, Lord, Please Excuse the Mess!
1. 2 Corinthians 12:7-9
2. *The Maximized Living Bible*, Dr. Ben Lerner, "The Power of Christ," 2017, p. 1273.
3. *The Maximized Living Bible*, Dr. Ben Lerner, "The Power of Christ," 2017, p. 1273.
4. *The Maximized Living Bible*, Dr. Ben Lerner, "The Power of Christ," 2017, p. 1273.
5. Matthew 8:8

Chapter 2: Taking Out the Trash
1. Genesis 31:19-35
2. *Where the Sidewalk Ends*, "Sarah Cynthia Sylvia Stout Would Not Take the Garbage Out," by Shel Silverstein, Harper Collins Publishers, 1974.
3. Ceci Garrett, professional clutter coach, Spokane County, Washington, www.facebook.com/CeciGarrett/

4. Genesis 31:34-35
5. Money Prodigy, www.moneyprodigy.com
6. Living on a Dime, www.livingonadime.com
7. Living on a Dime, www.livingonadime.com
8. Psychology Today, www.psychologytoday.com
9. The Spruce, www.thespruce.com

Chapter 3: Getting Started
1. Genesis 6:14-16
2. Exodus 25:1-31:11
3. Book of Nehemiah, chapters 1-5 & 6:1-15
4. Nehemiah 1:2-3
5. Nehemiah 1:2-4
6. Nehemiah 1:4-11
7. Nehemiah 2:4
8. Nehemiah 2:6
9. Nehemiah 2:7-8
10. Nehemiah 2:11-15
11. Nehemiah 1:6-7

Chapter 4: No More Shame
1. Isaiah 52:13-15 & Isaiah 53
2. Isaiah 54
3. Isaiah 39:2
4. Isaiah 39:6
5. Isaiah 39:8
6. Isaiah 39:8
7. Psalm 18:19

Chapter 5: Get More Done By working Together
1. Ceci Garrett, professional clutter coach, Spokane County, Washington, www.facebook.com/CeciGarrett/

Chapter 6: Don't Fall Off Your Stick
1. Discovery Channel, Skywire Live with Nik Wallenda, www.discovery.com/tv-shows/skywire-live-with-nik-wallenda/
2. Google: "Grand Canyon High-Wire Man Nik Wallenda THANKS JESUS! TMZ."
3. Google: Nik Wallenda Grand Canyon High-Wire Act—THANK YOU JESUS!—TMZ.com at www.tmz.com/2013/06/24/nik-wallenda-grand-canyon-high-wire
4. www.yourmodernfamily.com
5. Age of Montessori, www.ageofmontessori.org
6. www.moneyprodigy.com
7. Early Bird Mom, www.earlybirdmom.com

Chapter 7: From Immobilized to Energized
1. Isaiah 9:32-35.
2. *ADDitude—Inside the ADHD Mind*, "Face It: People with ADHD Are Wired Differently," by Oren Mason, M.D. and Tamara Rosier, Ph.D., www.additudemag.com/current-research-on-adhd-breakdown-of-the-adhd-brain/

3. *Medical News Today*, "ADHD: Large Imaging Study confirms Differences in several Brain Regions," by Catherine Paddock, Ph.D., Feb. 16, 2017, www.medicalnewstoday.com/articles/325884.php
4. *The Conversation*, "Imaging Study Confirms Differences in ADHD Brains," by Alison Poulton, Feb.19, 2017, www.theconversation.com/imaging-study-confirms-differences-in-adhd-brains-73117
5. Money Prodigy, www.moneyprodigy.com
6. The Happy Housewife, www.thehappyhousewife.com
7. Association for Comprehensive Neurotherapy, www.latitudes.org
8. 100 Things 2 Do, www.100things2do.ca
9. Focus on the Family, www.focusonthefamily.org
10. Psychology Today, www.psychologytoday.com

Chapter 8: Get Dressed

1. Money Prodigy, "Age Appropriate Chore for Kids," www.moneyprodigy.com/age-appropriate-chores-for-kids/
2. Family Life, "Age-Appropriate Chores for Children," from *Life Skills* for Kids, by Christine M. Field, Shaw Books, 2000, www.familylife.com/articles/topics/parenting/foundations/character-

development/age-appropriate-chores-for-children/
3. Focus on the Family Australia, "Age Appropriate Chores," by Dr. Bill Maier, www.families.org.au/article/age-appropriate-chores
4. Psychology Today, "Age-Appropriate Chores for Children," by Rebecca Jackson, Nov. 13, 2014, www.psychologytoday.com/us/blog/school-thought/201411/age-appropriate-chores-children

Chapter 9: The Sea of Clutter
1. Exodus 14:10-12
2. Exodus 14:15-16, 21-22
3. *Answers In Genesis*, "How Long Were the Israelites in Egypt?" by David Wright, July 5, 2010, www.answersingenesis.org/bible-questions/how-long-were-the-israelites-in-egypt/

Chapter 10: Call Me Blessed
1. Genesis 21:1-3
2. 1 Chronicles 1:34, Genesis 25:19-26, 1 Chronicles 2:1, Genesis 49:1-28
3. Luke 1:35
4. Luke 1:5-25

Chapter 12: Swept & Put in Order
1. Luke 11:24-26

2. *Very Well Family*, "Giving Kids Chore That Are Right for Their Age," by Katherine Lee, Aug.19, 2017, www.verywellfamily.com/giving-kids-chores-that-are-right-for-their-age-620310
3. *Focus on the Family*, "Age-Appropriate Chores: How to Help Kids Be Responsible,"by Sheila Seifert, www.focusonthefamily.com/parenting/parenting-challenges/motivating-kids-to-clean-up/age-appropriate-chores

Chapter 14: Defeating the Enemy
1. Tak Bhana, Church Unlimited, New Zealand, www.churchunlimited.co.nz/resources/blog/total-defeat-of-satan/
2. Ephesians 6:11, 13-17
3. Psalm 68:17b-18
4. Matthew 19:26

Chapter 15: When Clutter Becomes a Spiritual Battle
1. Nehemiah 4:12
2. Nehemiah 4:16-23
3. Ephesians 6:18
4. Nehemiah 6:9
5. Nehemiah 1:11

Chapter 16: Emotional Ties That Bind Us to Clutter
1. *Downsizing the Family Home*, by Marni Jameson, Sterling Publishing, 2015, p. 140.

2. *Downsizing the Family Home*, by Marni Jameson, Sterling Publishing, 2015, p. 141.
3. *Downsizing the Family Home*, by Marni Jameson, Sterling Publishing, 2015, p. 142.
4. *Buried in Treasures: Help for Compulsive Acquiring, Saving & Hoarding*, by David F. Tolin, Randy O. Frost and Gail Steketee, Oxford University Press, 2014.
5. Ceci Garrett, professional clutter coach, Spokane County, Washington, www.facebook.com/CeciGarrett/
6. *Downsizing the Family Home*, by Marni Jameson, Sterling Publishing, 2015, p. 142.

Chapter 17: "Fuh Gedd Bow Dit"
1. SimpLESSity Decluttering Program, www.alejandra.tv/training/how-to-declutter-program-simplessity/
2. *Downsizing the Family Home*, by Marni Jameson, Sterling Publishing, 2015, p. 150.

Chapter 18: From Avoidance to Forgiveness
1. Ceci Garrett, professional clutter coach, Spokane County, Washington, www.facebook.com/CeciGarrett/
2. *Buried in Treasures: Help for Compulsive Acquiring, Saving & Hoarding*, by David F. Tolin, Randy

O. Frost and Gail Steketee, Oxford University Press, 2014.
3. Mark Brunetz, clutter-free living expert, quoted in *Downsizing the Family Home*, by Marni Jameson, Sterling Publishing, 2015, p. 144.
4. Psalm 103:12
5. Life Services, Spokane, Washington, Post-Abortion Care, www.lifeservices.org/services/post-abortion-care/

Chapter 19: Can't Take It with You
1. Psalm 143:8b

Chapter 20: More Than Enough
1. Genesis 22:1-14
2. Exodus 36:3-5
3. Exodus 36:21-29

Chapter 21: Physical Preparedness v. Spiritual Readiness
1. Genesis 1:26-27, 9:6
2. Genesis 41:29-30, 33-36, 47-49
3. Proverbs 30:25

Chapter 23: A Pile to Remind Us
1. Genesis 31:44-52
2. Genesis 29:20-28, 30:25-43, 31:6, 14-15, 17-22, 26-27, 30-35, 38-41

Chapter 24: I Have Everything I Need
1. Genesis 33:9-11, New Century Version
2. www.facebook.com/watch/?v=321565655062991
3. www.facebook.com/DailyHealthPost/photos/a.647186735296191.1073741829.533986213282911/1384924938189030/?type=3
4. www.facebook.com/watch/?v=10153665590087371
5. www.facebook.com/TheRealChristianMinistry/posts/1642364415809436

Chapter 25: The Wilderness of Sin
1. Numbers 33:11-12 & Exodus 16:1
2. Smith's Bible Dictionary, Dr. William Smith, "Entry for 'Sin, Wilderness of,'" 1901, www.biblestudytools.com/dictionaries/smiths-bible-dictionary/sin-wilderness-of.html
3. Illustrated Bible Dictionary, Third Edition, M.G. Easton M.A., D.D., Thomas Nelson, 1897. www.biblestudytools.com/dictionaries/eastons-bible-dictionary/sin-wilderness-of.html
4. Exodus 17:1a, ESV

MORE RESOURCES FOR SPIRITUAL HEALING AND RECOVERY

Abortion Anonymous, Inc.—Abortion Anonymous (AbAnon) is a Non-Profit Organization whose mission is to assist women and men through the process of healing the emotional pain brought on from a past abortion. www.abanon.org, https://www.facebook.com/abortionanonymous, m.me/abortionanonymous, confidential email: joinus@abanon.org.

Abortion Recovery InterNational (ARIN) http://abortionrecovery.org, 1-866-4-My-Recovery.

ARIN CARE (Compassion Abortion Recovery Effort) Directory—to locate the closest Recovery CARE

Center/Program in your area. Abortion Recovery InterNational's CARE Directory is an online listing of ARIN Partners who provide personal, confidential and non-judgmental assistance to those hurting from a past abortion. http://abortionrecovery.org/recovery/CARE-directory/tabid/234/Default.aspx

Abortion Recovery CARE Line—To talk to an Abortion Recovery Consultant or for help locating abortion recovery care assistance in your area, call: 1-866-721-7781.

AfterAbortion.com—A politically neutral site devoted to healing and recovery for women who've had abortions. This site does not endorse any political view about abortion, or endorse any specific religious view about abortion. It is strictly a neutral place of healing, information and support for women, their families and friends after an abortion.

A.R.T.S. Anonymous—Artists Recovering through the Twelve Steps—A 12-step program for multi-talented, avoidant, or creatively blocked artists who struggle with perfectionism, fear (of criticism, rejection, failure, or success)—for whom creative work is started but not finished, or whose completed work is abandoned. The goal in A.R.T.S. is to achieve an active, abundant and robust creative life. A.R.T.S. is a fellowship of artists who are taking daily actions to achieve their goals. Website: www.artsanonymous.org

Buried in Treasures: Help for Compulsive Acquiring, Saving, and Hoarding, by Dr. David Tolin, Dr. Randy O. Frost, and Dr. Gail Steketee, Oxford University Press, USA, 2nd edition, November 15, 2013.

Ceci Garrett, Christian writer/speaker, & professional coach/consultant on clutter & hoarding tendencies, & in-home therapeutic decluttering, https://www.facebook.com/CeciGarrett/ .

Celebrate Recovery—A Christ-centered, 12-step recovery program for anyone struggling with hurt, pain or addiction of any kind. https://www.celebraterecovery.com

Resources for Help After Abortion—To find Abortion After-Care Programs in your area. http://www.silentnomoreawareness.org/search/index.aspx

GRATITUDE

First and foremost, I am grateful for the loving support of my best friend and husband, John, who has been patiently waiting over fifteen years for this book to be written and published.

I am beyond grateful for the invaluable help of my coaches—Ceci Garrett, Gary Williams, and Lise Cartwright, and for the work of my gem of an editor—Bonita Jewel, as well as for the entire SPS Authors Community—especially my dear accountability partners, Ann and Monika—all of whom came alongside me every step of the way through this book writing and publishing journey. I could not have done any of this without this amazing community of authors.

Most of all, though, I am grateful to my Lord and Savior, Jesus Christ, without whom I am nothing.

And, last but not least, I am grateful to you, dear reader, for reading my book. I would love to stay in touch. Feel free to email me at Cassandra@CassandraTiersma.com, and let me know how this book has impacted you and your life, or what other related topics you would like to read about in my upcoming books.

ABOUT THE AUTHOR

Cassandra Tiersma is a self-confessed Messy-a.n.i.c. (messy, absentminded, normal-ish, imperfect, creative) Christian author and professional freelance writer/reporter who's had well over a hundred of her articles published in newspapers. Blessed with a loud and infectious laugh, and an accidental "ministry of laughter," Cassandra has been known to be a fool for Christ—whether in writing and performing comedic monologues or song parodies, teaching kids' dance classes, or singing, and playing her antique autoharp.

Cassandra has been leading the way for other women throughout her life—as a performance artist, writer, speaker, workshop presenter, and ministry leader. It is Cassandra's mission to bless and encourage other Messy-a.n.i.c. Christian women in their faith, so that they can become the full expression of who God created them to be.

Cassandra lives with her husband in a small town in the frontier territory of the mythological 51st State of Jefferson, where she serves as women's ministry director at the historic little stone chapel that is their church home.

Cassandra loves to hear from her readers. She can be reached at Cassandra@CassandraTiersma.com.

Can you help?

If you found any part of this book helpful in your own Messy-a.n.i.c. walk, or you have noticed other Messy-a.n.i.c. Christian women benefit from this study, please go online and post an honest review of ***Come In, Lord, Please Excuse the Mess!*** at Amazon.com.

Thank you!

Made in the USA
Las Vegas, NV
20 October 2024